THE SCIENCE OF SEEDS

WHY WE EAT MAIZE, WHEAT, RICE, AND POTATOES

**WITH HANDS-ON
SCIENCE ACTIVITIES
FOR KIDS**

CARLA MOONEY
ILLUSTRATED BY
MICAH RAUCH

More science titles from Nomad Press

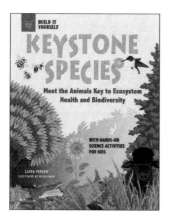

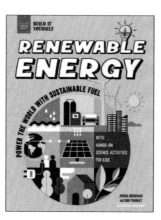

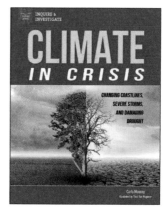

Check out more titles at www.nomadpress.net

Nomad Press

A division of Nomad Communications

10 9 8 7 6 5 4 3 2 1

This book was manufactured by Versa Press, East Peoria, Illinois
June 2024, Job #J24-50809

ISBN Softcover: 978-1-64741-115-2
ISBN Hardcover: 978-1-64741-112-1

Educational Consultant, Marla Conn

Questions regarding the ordering of this book should be addressed to
Nomad Press
PO Box 1036, Norwich, VT 05055
www.nomadpress.net

Printed in the United States.

CONTENTS

**Interested in
Primary Sources?
Look for this icon.**

Some of the QR codes in this book link to primary sources that offer firsthand information about the topic. Many photos are considered primary sources as well because a photograph takes a picture at the moment something happens. Use a smartphone or tablet app to scan the QR code and explore more! You can find a list of the URLs on the Resources page. You can also use the suggested keywords to find other helpful sources.

🔎 seeds

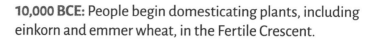

10,000 BCE: People begin domesticating plants, including einkorn and emmer wheat, in the Fertile Crescent.

8000 to 7000 BCE: Wild teosinte grows in the Americas. People begin domesticating teosinte into a crop that will eventually become maize.

7000 to 6000 BCE: Chinese farmers begin to domesticate rice.

8000 to 5000 BCE: Farmers begin to domesticate potatoes in the Andes Mountains of South America.

2000 BCE to 900 CE: Maya civilization, fueled by maize, reaches its peak.

468 BCE: The Chinese build the Grand Canal to transport rice and other materials between southern and northern regions.

1200 CE: The Inca form a kingdom in the Andes Mountains and begin building an empire with the potato as a staple food.

1325: The Aztec found the city of Tenochtitlan on the site of today's Mexico City and rely on maize to feed their population.

1493: European explorer Christopher Columbus returns to Europe with maize.

1500s: Maize and potatoes spread through Europe. European explorers bring wheat and rice to the Americas.

Early 1800s: The U.S. Secretary of the Treasury directs U.S. ambassadors and military officers to gather seeds and seed data from their posts worldwide.

1800s: The Industrial Revolution brings new machines that make farming more efficient, including the mechanical reaper, mechanical thresher, and steel plow.

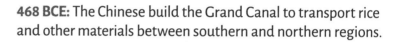

1845: The potato blight reaches Ireland, and the Irish Potato Famine begins. It lasts until 1851. Millions of people die or flee the country.

Early 1900s: Maize shows become a popular social event in the U.S. Corn Belt.

1920s: Russian agricultural scientist Nikolai Vavilov researches crop centers of origin. He creates the world's first seed bank in Leningrad in the Soviet Union.

1922: The first hybrid maize is produced and sold commercially.

1940s: American scientist Norman Borlaug develops a new hybrid wheat variety that is able to produce higher yields and resist disease. The Green Revolution begins a period of initiatives to greatly increase crop yields and production.

1960: The International Rice Research Institute is formed and begins work on a hybrid rice plant that will produce higher yields. It creates IR8, which is nicknamed the "miracle rice" and significantly increases yields.

1990s: The first genetically modified organism (GMO) crops, including maize and potatoes, are created through genetic engineering.

2008: The Svalbard Global Seed Vault opens in Norway.

2010s: Independent seed companies emerge to meet the increasing demand for organic seeds in the United States.

2021: The United States is the world's largest producer of maize, producing 15.1 billion bushels.

2023: About 75 percent of the world's food comes from just 12 plant and five animal species.

HOW DOES A SEED GROW?

Everything a plant needs to grow is inside its seed—just add light, warmth, and nutrients! Inside the seed, a part called the **embryo** contains the **radicle**, **plumule**, and **cotyledons**. The radicle becomes the plant's first root. The plumule grows as the plant's first shoot, which becomes the stem. The cotyledons are the plant's first leaves. They contain enough food for the young plant to survive until it has plenty of leaves to produce its own food through **photosynthesis**.

Photosynthesis is how plants convert light into energy. They also need water and carbon dioxide. And their waste product? Oxygen! That's why plants and trees are vital to all other life on earth—and to the health of the planet.

When it grows into an adult, the plant will have flower blossoms to attract pollinators to fertilize new seeds and the life cycle will continue!

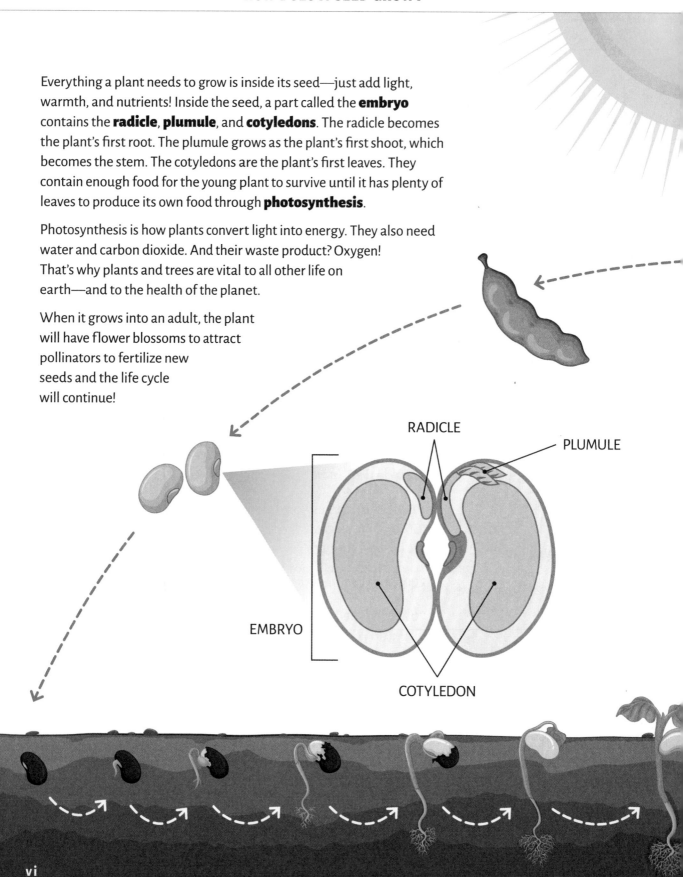

RADICLE

PLUMULE

EMBRYO

COTYLEDON

HOW DOES A SEED GROW?

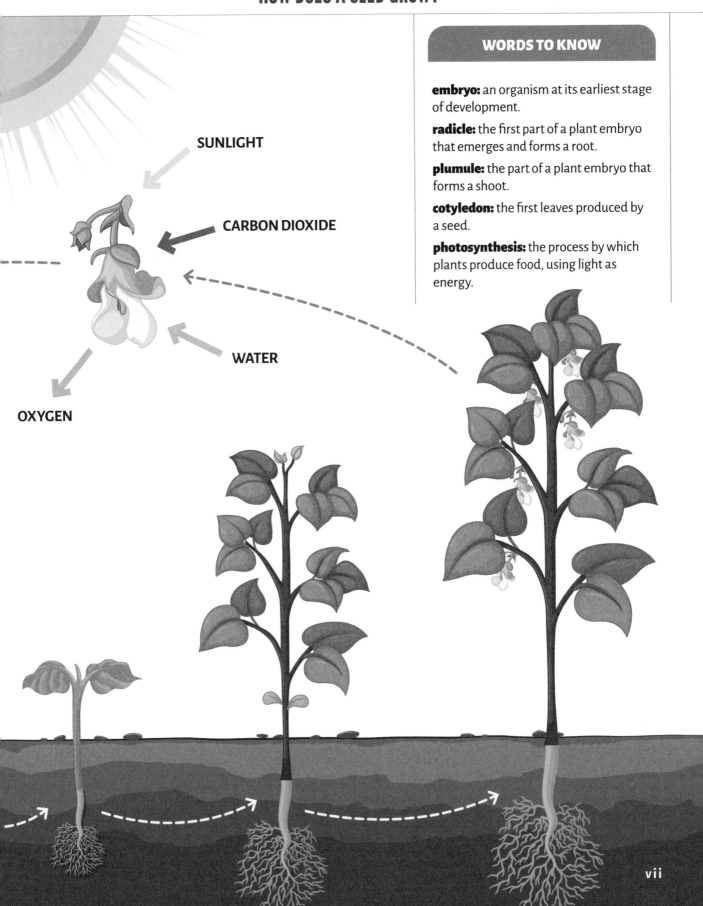

SUNLIGHT

CARBON DIOXIDE

WATER

OXYGEN

WORDS TO KNOW

embryo: an organism at its earliest stage of development.

radicle: the first part of a plant embryo that emerges and forms a root.

plumule: the part of a plant embryo that forms a shoot.

cotyledon: the first leaves produced by a seed.

photosynthesis: the process by which plants produce food, using light as energy.

SEEDS, SEEDS,
EVERYWHERE!

Maize, wheat, rice, and potatoes. From Lagos to Los Angeles, these four **staple foods** can be found in our breakfast cereals, lunch boxes, and on our dinner tables. The foods we love would not be the same without these four staple foods. What would a Rice Krispie Treat taste like without rice? Without potatoes, you would have no crispy French fries to dip in ketchup. And your burrito would be hard to hold without corn or wheat to make tortillas! How did we come to rely so much on these four foods?

Since our earliest days, plants have been essential to the human diet. Today, we have more than 50,000 **edible** plant species on Earth, an incredible **diversity**. Yet only a few hundred plants make up a significant part of our diet. And just 15 plants provide 90 percent of the **calories** we eat. Of those, "the big four" **crops**—maize, wheat, rice, and potatoes—are staple foods for about 5 billion people. These big four crops are stable and widespread. Even in changing **climate** conditions, we rely on them to feed the majority of humans.

ESSENTIAL QUESTION

Why do we rely on so few staple crops in a world of agricultural diversity?

1

maize: a Central American cereal plant, also known as corn.

staple food: a food that is an essential part of our diet.

edible: can be eaten.

diversity: a range of different people or things.

calorie: a unit of energy in food.

crops: plants grown for food and other uses.

climate: the long-term weather pattern in a region.

nutrition: the vitamins, minerals, and other things in food that your body uses to stay healthy and grow.

agriculture: the science or practice of farming.

malnutrition: poor nutrition caused by not eating the right foods.

nutrient: a substance in food and soil that living things need to live and grow.

WHAT ARE STAPLE FOODS?

A staple food is a food that is a significant part of a population's diet. People eat staple foods regularly, often daily. These foods provide a large portion of the calories and **nutrition** a person needs.

Many staple foods come from plants. They are inexpensive and provide a lot of calories to give us energy. Beyond maize, wheat, rice, and potatoes, other staple foods include millet, sorghum, cassava, and yams. Not all staple foods are plants. Animal products such as meat, fish, and dairy are also staple foods.

A staple food in one region may not be as crucial for people living in another region. For example, millet, rice, and soybeans are staple foods in China. In Mexico, maize and potatoes are more common staple foods. For centuries, a region's staple foods were linked to the plants and crops that could grow nearby.

However, improvements in **agriculture** and transportation now allow staple foods to spread to new places worldwide. Have you ever had quinoa? Quinoa is a grain-like plant grown in the Andes Mountains in South America. Today, people as far away as North America, Europe, Asia, and Africa enjoy eating quinoa.

Staple foods are nutritious but do not provide *all* the nutrition people need. To avoid malnutrition, people must eat foods with other nutrients.

The Scientific Method

A scientific method worksheet is a useful tool for keeping your ideas and observations organized. The scientific method is the process scientists use to ask and answer questions. Use a notebook as a science journal to make a scientific method worksheet for each experiment.

Question: What are we trying to find out? What problem are we trying to solve?

Research: What is already known about this topic?

Hypothesis: What do we think the answer will be?

Equipment: What supplies are we using?

Method: What procedure are we following?

Results: What happened and why?

credit: International Rice Research Institute (CC BY 2.0)

THE SCIENCE OF SEEDS

WORDS TO KNOW

evolution: gradual change across many years.

civilization: a complex human society.

cultivate: to raise and grow plants for food.

hunter-gatherer: a nomadic person who lives by hunting, fishing, and collecting food.

forage: to search widely for food.

proteins: nutrients that are essential to the growth and repair of cells in the body.

fats: nutrients that are essential to give your body energy and support cell function.

carbohydrates: nutrients that are an important source of energy.

nomadic: a lifestyle that involves moving from place to place.

anthropologist: a scientist who studies humans and human behavior.

harvest: to gather crops.

environment: everything in nature, living and nonliving, including plants, animals, soil, rocks, and water.

germinate: to sprout or begin to grow.

A CONNECTED HISTORY

The big four staple foods do more than feed people worldwide. These top crops have also played a role in the **evolution** of human **civilization**. The history of humans and the crops we grow have been interconnected for thousands of years.

Staple foods supported the first human civilizations—wheat and barley in the Near East, rice and millet in Asia, and maize and potatoes in the Americas. And they did not grow by accident. Instead, humans purposely **cultivated** these crops. In doing so, people transformed these crops from wild plants into the staple foods we enjoy today. And with these crops, our human ancestors evolved from hunters and gatherers to early farmers. These changes took place slowly across many generations.

LIFE AS A HUNTER-GATHERER

Hunting and gathering was a way of life for most of human history. In fact, until about 12,000 years ago, all humans were **hunter-gatherers**. Hunter-gatherers hunted and fished for meat. They **foraged** for plants, seeds, berries, fruits, and vegetables to eat. Hunter-gatherers ate a variety of foods that contained a wide range of nutrients. Meats, fish, and plants provided **proteins**, **fats**, **carbohydrates**, and nutrients.

TEXT TO **WORLD**

Imagine what your life would be like as a hunter-gatherer. How would you find food where you live? What could you hunt or fish? What plants could you gather to eat?

Hunter-gatherers were very active. They traveled across large areas of land to find the food they needed. They were **nomadic**. But imagine if your entire neighborhood had to travel together all the time to gather food—that's too many people! Nomadic groups had to be smaller. Some included only the members of an extended family. Others were larger and included multiple families. However, few groups had more than about 100 people.

Anthropologists and other scientists who have studied hunter-gatherer groups believe they accumulated a vast knowledge of the natural world. And they used that knowledge to survive. They could identify edible plants and knew which parts of the plant could be eaten. They understood when plants sprouted, bloomed, and were ready to **harvest**. They knew when animals and birds mated and had their young. They were able to extract medicines and poisons from plants. They used plant fibers to make clothing, baskets, and other objects.

As early as about 12,000 years ago, humans lived on all continents except Antarctica.

Hunter-gatherers also learned to manage their **environment**. For example, they set controlled fires to eliminate weeds and insects. The fires also helped seeds with hard shells such as pine nuts, chestnuts, and walnuts to **germinate**. More germinating seeds meant more seed-producing, edible plants. After the fires, new grass grew and attracted animals for grazing.

ADOPTING AGRICULTURE

For thousands of years, humans survived by hunting, fishing, and foraging. Then, about 12,000 years ago, evidence shows that nomadic human tribes began to use tools that allowed them to grow and cultivate their food. The gradual adoption of agriculture and farming has enormously impacted our human story.

THE SCIENCE OF SEEDS

WORDS TO KNOW

tuber: the thick part of the stem, usually developed underground, of certain plants such as potatoes.

domesticate: to adapt a plant or animal from a wild state to benefit humans.

migrate: to move from one region to another.

With agriculture, early humans no longer needed to travel far and wide for food. The traditional hunter-gatherer lifestyle, which humans had always followed, was slowly replaced. Humans grew crops and had a reliable food source. Permanent settlements were established near farmlands.

As time went on, settlements grew into towns and cities. And because farms could produce enough food to feed more people, the number of people skyrocketed. About 10,000 years ago, about 5 million people lived on Earth. Today, more than 8 billion humans live on our planet.

Scientists cannot point to a single reason why hunter-gatherer groups adopted farming. Another mystery is how people living in different parts of the world, who had no contact with each other, independently adopted agriculture. In the Near East, evidence of early farming of wheat dates back 11,000 to 12,000 years. People began growing rice 9,000 years ago in China's Yellow River Valley. African people grew **tubers** and roots around 5,000 to 8,000 years ago. And in South America, people began growing maize, beans, and squash between 7,000 and 9,000 years ago.

The Hadza of Tanzania

In Africa, the Hadza people of northern Tanzania still rely on hunting and gathering to survive. They have no **domesticated** livestock and do not grow their own food. Instead, they hunt game with handmade bows and arrows and forage for tubers, plants, and honey. Because they follow a nomadic lifestyle, they do not have permanent homes. Instead, the Hadza build temporary shelters from dried grass and branches. They own few possessions, which makes it easier to move to a new camp. Today, there are about 1,300 Hadza tribe members. They are one of the last hunter-gatherer tribes in Africa.

Ancient Egyptians used oxen to help with the work of growing and harvesting food.

A TURNING POINT

The gradual shift from hunting and gathering to agriculture was a turning point in human history. In places across the globe, people without contact with each other began to grow crops. They grew crops suited to their specific climate and environment. When they **migrated** to new regions, they brought their crops and seeds with them. As they met new people, groups began to trade with each other. Seeds, crops, and agriculture spread to new places.

The story of top crops—maize, wheat, rice, and potatoes—is closely intertwined with early humans and their first agricultural efforts. Where did these crops come from? How did humans cultivate them? And how did these crops become so important to human history? Let's investigate and find out how these crops came to shape our world.

WHAT'S IN THE
PANTRY?

Maize, wheat, rice, and potatoes are four of the most common staple crops in the world. But how common are these foods in your home? How much of what you like to eat depends on these four top crops?

> Take an inventory of the food in your kitchen pantry, cabinets, and refrigerator. Make a list of everything you find.

> After you have your list of food, place each into a food category: corn, wheat, rice, or potato. You can add some additional categories, such as dairy, fruits and vegetables, and meat. Look at the list of ingredients on boxes and cans to determine if they contain any staple foods.

> Once you have sorted the food by category, think about the following questions.

✱ What staple food did you find the most?

✱ What staple food did you find the least?

✱ Did you find any foods that did not fit into any of your categories? What were they?

> Based on what you found, consider how much your family relies on staple foods. Is it a lot?

Consider This!

If one of the four top crops was no longer available, what foods would you not be able to eat? How would you replace these foods in your diet? What substitutions could you make?

Essential Questions

Each chapter of this book begins with an essential question to help guide your exploration of seeds. Keep the question in your mind as you read the chapter. At the end of each chapter, use your science journal to record your thoughts and answers.

ESSENTIAL QUESTION

Why do we rely on so few staple crops in a world of agricultural diversity?

FIRST FARMERS,
FIRST CROPS

Ask any farmer and they'll tell you: Farming is a lot of work. It takes a lot of planning and labor to SOW, weed, plant, harvest, process, and store crops. Why did we start doing it in the first place? For thousands of years, humans were successful hunter-gatherers. Why did they abandon the hunter-gatherer life to become farmers?

For thousands of years, early humans survived on plants and animals that they gathered and hunted. Only within the past 12,000 years have humans begun to grow or cultivate food on purpose. And farming did not start in one place. Instead, it emerged in several different regions and times, independent of each other. From these origin points, farming gradually spread throughout the world.

ESSENTIAL QUESTION

Why did humans start cultivating crops in different parts of the world at about the same time?

THE SCIENCE OF SEEDS

Why did early humans turn to farming? That is one of the oldest questions in human history! This question has puzzled anthropologists for years. To understand, modern anthropologists have studied the few remaining hunter-gatherer groups on Earth. By doing so, they have learned some interesting information.

First, gathering food takes much less time and effort than farming. The !Kung Bushmen are hunter-gatherers who live in the Kalahari Desert in southern Africa. They spend about 12 to 19 hours a week gathering food.

The Hazda are another group of nomadic hunter-gatherers in Tanzania. The Hazda spend less than 14 hours a week gathering food. That is the equivalent of working two seven-hour days and having the rest of the week off. Anthropologists believe that it is unlikely that early humans turned to farming so they could have more free time.

A Hazda hunter near Lake Eyasi, Tanzania

credit: A_Peach from Berlin, Germany (CC BY 2.0)

You can see some of the Hazda lifestyle in this video. How are their lives different from yours? How are they similar? **Please be aware this video has graphic moments.**

🔎 Nat Geo Hadza video

PS

Another theory is that early farmers began farming to create a **stable** food source. For the most part, you don't have to worry about finding your next meal if you grow crops. A steady food source would keep early humans well-fed. They would have less malnutrition and related diseases.

Humans get 60 percent of their calories from three plant species— maize, rice, and wheat.

Yet scientists have found evidence that the opposite might be true. Hunter-gatherers might have been healthier than early farmers. Why do we think this? Modern Bushmen eat about 75 wild plants instead of only a few staple crops. The variety of their diet provides a full range of essential vitamins, minerals, and other nutrients. **Archaeologists**, who study ancient people and their **cultures**, have studied the skeletal remains of early humans. The skeletons of early farmers were shorter than those of hunter-gatherers. This suggests the farmers suffered from malnutrition. The bones of early farmers also showed evidence of diseases such as scurvy and rickets, which are caused by a lack of vitamins in their diet.

THE SCIENCE OF SEEDS

WORDS TO KNOW

Ice Age: a period of time when glaciers covered a large part of the earth.

savanna: a large grassy area with few trees.

herbivore: an animal that eats only plants.

drought: a long period of dry weather, especially one that damages crops.

natural selection: one of the basic means of evolution in which organisms that are well-adapted to their environment are better able to survive, reproduce, and pass along their useful traits to offspring.

organism: something living, such as a plant or an animal.

adapt: to change in order to survive.

reproduce: to make more of something.

species: a group of living things that are closely related and can produce offspring.

breed: to develop new types of plants and animals with improved characteristics.

artificial selection: the breeding of plants and animals to produce desired traits.

predator: an animal that hunts and eats other animals.

fertilize: to add something to soil to make crops grow better.

pesticide: a chemical used to kill pests on crops.

ADAPTING TO A CHANGING CLIMATE

Some scientists believe that changes in Earth's climate may have caused the gradual shift from hunting and gathering to farming. According to climate scientists, Earth's most recent **Ice Age** lasted until about 11,500 years ago. During an ice age, thick sheets of ice covered enormous areas of land. The climate was cold, dry, and unstable. In these conditions, consistently growing plants would have been tough. Even if hunter-gatherers tried to grow plants, extreme climate might have caused the crops to fail.

As the Ice Age ended, Earth's climate became warmer, wetter, and more stable. Conditions improved for growing wild plants. Early people who gathered wild grains might have started planting some seeds to grow more food.

In some areas, the changing climate could have made it more difficult for hunter-gatherers to find food. For example, in Southwest Asia and Africa, rainfall decreased and drought set in. Some plant and animal species could not survive in the new environment.

The lack of rain also turned rainforests into **savannas** during many years. **Herbivore** animals now had to move to new lands for grazing. There was no longer enough food—either plants or animals—for people living in these savannas to survive. Perhaps they were forced to try growing wild grains to provide essential food.

Planting seeds might have been a way to ensure they had enough food when other food sources were scarce.

During frequent **droughts**, early humans began to camp closer to lakes and ponds so they could be sure of having enough water. They could also hunt the animals that came to the water to drink. Traditionally, the women of the group did the foraging. Now, they spread wild grass seeds in nearby marshes and riverbanks. Some people planted parts of tubers to grow new plants.

Approximately 30,000 plant species are used in medicine.

Archaeological evidence suggests that people first grew whatever wild cereal grains were nearby. They gathered seeds from wild plants and planted them to grow new ones. However, some grains produced more food than others. As time passed, people began to choose the grains that produced the most food for the same amount of work.

Artificial Selection

In nature, the process of **natural selection** is part of evolution. **Organisms** that **adapt** to their environment are more likely to survive and **reproduce**. They pass on the genes that help them survive to their offspring. Through natural selection, **species** adapt and change through time.

When humans domesticated certain plant species, they interfered with nature's process of natural selection. People chose traits they preferred in the plants to **breed**, regardless of whether the traits helped the plants survive. This process is called **artificial selection**.

Artificial selection has made some plants more vulnerable to disease, **predators**, and environmental stress. As a result, these domesticated plants struggle to survive without human help. Today, farmers **fertilize** and water crops to encourage growth. They spray with **pesticides** to protect against disease and predators. Domesticated crops need humans to survive. And humans rely on these crops for survival as well.

WORDS TO KNOW

pest: a destructive insect or other animal that attacks crops, food, and livestock.

parasite: an organism that feeds on and lives in another organism.

fertile: good for growing crops.

SETTLING DOWN

Gradually, hunter-gatherers began to rely more on plants and farming. Less and less frequently, they traveled across great distances to hunt and gather. Instead, they began to spend more time at a single camp, probably in a place where crops grew well. Some groups built permanent homes.

Staying in one place for longer meant the people did not have to carry their belongings from camp to camp. At the time, humans used grinding stones to process wild grains. In more permanent homes, people no longer needed to move the stones and other heavy tools. Wild grains could also be dried and stored for long periods. Staying in one place made it easier to rely more on wild grains for food.

As early humans settled down, the size of their groups grew. One reason for this is because women began having more children. Hunter-gatherers carried everything from camp to camp, including babies.

Nomadic women carried their children until they could walk long distances on their own, usually around age three or four. Only when her child could walk a long ways on their own did a nomadic woman consider having another child. By staying in one place, they did not have to wait to have more children. As women began having more babies, the population grew. More mouths to feed! The need for more food likely led the group to plant more crops. In time, farming became the community's primary source of food.

In time, weeds, pests, and parasites can invade farmland and make it less productive. Farmers are always looking for ways to keep their land healthy and fertile.

Most scientists believe this transition from hunting and gathering to farming happened slowly. Early people did not consciously decide to change their way of life. Instead, they most likely made changes to survive. If wild food sources were scarce, it made sense to plant a few seeds to increase the food supply. Gradually, they came to rely more and more on cultivated crops. At some point, they needed to farm to survive. It took many years and generations before the transition to agriculture was complete.

Where does our food come from?
Use this interactive map to explore where food crops were initially domesticated.

🔍 CIAT origin crops

DOMESTICATION OF PLANTS

Farming is unique to humans. Many animals gather and store seeds and other food. However, only humans deliberately planted and grew specific crops. And they did much more than that. Humans domesticated plants to better meet their needs. Certain crops changed forever because of human efforts. And the crops changed the course of human history.

THE SCIENCE OF SEEDS

Domestication is the process of making a species of wild plant or animal more useful for humans. With domesticated plants, people could grow more reliable, more useful crops. Domestication of plants began around 10,000 to 12,000 years ago in the **Fertile Crescent**, a region in western Asia and North Africa. We'll learn more about this region in Chapter 3. Some of the earliest domesticated plants included einkorn wheat, barley, chickpeas, lentils, and flax.

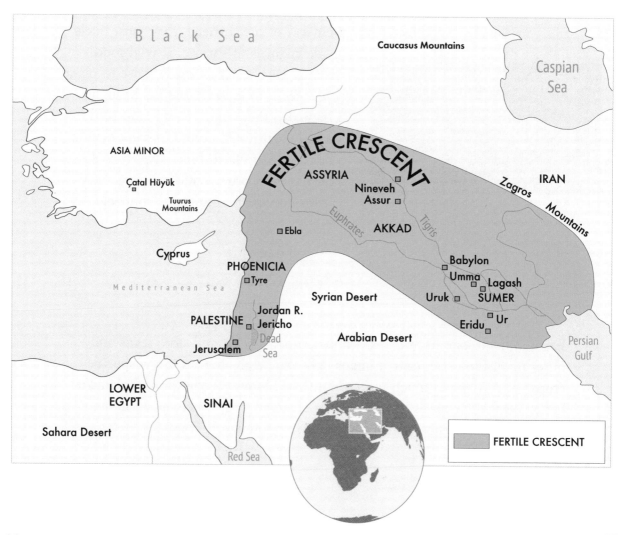

With domesticated plants, humans began to have more control over what they ate, where they moved, and how they lived.

At first, early humans chose wild plants that were good food sources. They gathered the plants' seeds and planted them. With time, people noticed some plants had more desirable **traits** than others. Some plants tasted better or grew bigger than others. Some plants were more resistant to pests. Some grew better in certain climates. People took the seeds from plants with desirable traits. They planted those seeds to grow the next crop. This process slowly produced more plants with the traits people wanted. With time, the domesticated plants became very different from the original wild plants.

Two in every five plant species is at risk of extinction.

Domesticated plants provided a reliable and plentiful source of food. Some of them, such as cotton and flax, could be used to make clothing. Domesticated animals such as cows, pigs, and sheep meant people needed to hunt less. Animal-based food sources, such as milk, were more readily available. In addition, domesticated animals, including horses and oxen, carried people and goods, while dogs and cats became human companions.

Watch this video to learn about the lives of five farmers of different ages in Ohio. How are their lives similar or different than your life? What would it be like to grow up in one of these families?

Our Ohio Life Farmer

The domestication of plants and animals was a significant event in human history. It marked the beginning of an agricultural way of life. Humans no longer needed to roam vast regions to hunt animals and gather plants.

They could establish more permanent communities. Domestication of plants created abundant new food sources. It also allowed some people to live a more **sedentary** lifestyle. Agriculture, which is the practice of farming, made it possible for fewer people to provide more food. Some people farmed. Others were able to perform different jobs.

THE SCIENCE OF SEEDS

WORDS TO KNOW

slash-and-burn agriculture: farming that uses fire to clear land for crops.

life cycle: the growth and changes a living thing goes through, from birth to death.

variation: a different form of something.

center of origin: the region where a crop was originally domesticated.

genetic diversity: the variety of genes within a species.

Having a predictable, reliable source of food made communities more stable. Populations grew. The first villages and cities emerged near fields of domesticated crops.

Thousands of years after the first farmers domesticated the first crops, many people still farm. Agriculture remains one of the largest and most essential industries in the modern world.

THE TOOLS OF FARMING

Have you ever visited a farm? There's a lot of machinery! Early farmers did not have the tractors and harvesting machines of today's farms. Instead, they used hand tools made from stone and animal bones.

They also used fire. To clear the land for farming, they first slashed any vegetation. Then, they set fires to burn a small clearing. After the fires burned out, the people planted seeds in the ashes. This method of farming is known as **slash-and-burn agriculture**. It creates a fertile plot of land for farming. Slash-and-burn agriculture is still used in parts of the Amazon rainforest, some forested hills of Southeast Asia, and in coastal West Africa.

Watch this short video about genetic diversity. Why is genetic diversity important for crops?

🔎 Convention Biological Diversity genetic

Later, people developed metal farming tools. Eventually, they designed plows pulled by domesticated animals. These improved tools allowed farmers to produce a lot more food, more than their families needed. At this point, farming appeared to have advantages over hunting and gathering. And for the first time, a human society emerged that was built on the division of labor.

AGRICULTURE AROUND THE WORLD

Agriculture emerged independently in different regions of the world. However, farming was easier in some places than it was in others. And different crops grew better in different areas, just like today. For example, in South America, people could grow tubers such as yams and potatoes. They learned to bury a small part of the tuber in the ground, and a new plant sprouted. They did not need to understand the plant's **life cycle** to grow identical plants. These groups quickly learned how to plant many types of tubers.

As humans began to travel and migrate to new places, they brought along their domesticated crops. In new environments, crops continued to adapt and evolve. But plants that grew well in one location did not always thrive in a new climate and environment. Would a desert cactus thrive in a rainforest?

Crop domestication led to crops with desirable traits. Across generations, the natural **variation** in some plants slowly decreased. Domestication also led to the loss of many valuable traits in the plants. Plants became less equipped to resist disease or adapt to changing conditions. As variation declined, the risk of a widespread crop failure increased. For example, the Great Famine of 1315–1317 was caused by unusually cold and rainy growing seasons in Europe, when grain and other crops could not ripen in fields.

CENTERS OF DIVERSITY

In the 1920s, Russian agricultural scientist Nikolai Vavilov (1887–1943) researched the idea of crop **centers of origin**. Vavilov believed he could identify where a crop was domesticated—its center of origin—by finding the region with the crop's greatest **genetic diversity**. Genetic diversity is the range of different inherited traits in a species.

THE SCIENCE OF SEEDS

A species with high genetic diversity would have many individuals with different traits. For example, there are more than 50,000 genetic varieties of rice worldwide.

Vavilov reasoned that farmers in that region would have been selecting different versions of the crop for the longest period of time. In the center of origin, scientists would also be able to find some remaining wild versions of the crop. Vavilov believed this, along with diversity, marked the crop's center of origin—its birthplace.

Between 1908 and 1940, Vavilov traveled around the world. He collected seeds, tubers, and roots of many plants. Vavilov led nearly 100 trips to countries on five continents. He traveled to Iran, Afghanistan, the United States, Central and South America, the Mediterranean, and Ethiopia. During this period, Vavilov built the world's most extensive plant **germplasm** collection.

Based on his research, Vavilov identified several areas as crop centers of origin. In these places, humans first cultivated a particular crop. The crop's ancestors, wild relatives, and related species still grow there.

Vavilov's centers of origin include China, India, Central Asia, the Near East, the Mediterranean, Ethiopia, southern Mexico and Central America, and South America.

Vavilov's collection included 350,000 samples of seeds, roots, and tubers for about 2,500 plants.

Other researchers continued Vavilov's work. They identified an additional center of origin in New Guinea. Today, scientists refer to these places as "centers of diversity" instead of "centers of origin." Scientists can determine a crop's center of **biodiversity** with data but can only make an educated guess at its true center of origin.

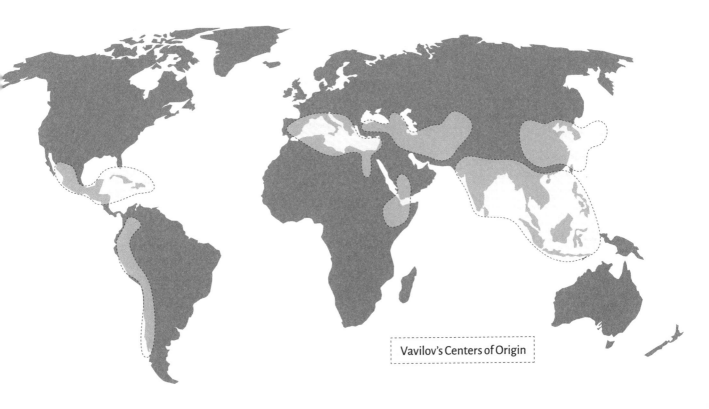

Vavilov's Centers of Origin

THE WORLD'S FIRST SEED BANK

In the 1920s, Vavilov created the world's first **seed bank** in Leningrad in the Soviet Union, now known as Russia. There, he stored his collections of seeds and germplasm, which included more than 300,000 seed varieties and germplasm of 2,500 plant species. At the seed bank, scientists performed experiments and researched the major crop varieties.

Russian postage stamp showing Nikolai Vavilov.

THE SCIENCE OF SEEDS

During World War II, German leader Adolf Hitler (1889–1945) was very interested in **genetics**. He ordered a special commando squad to capture Vavilov's seed bank. In June 1941, German forces invaded the Soviet Union.

The seed bank also faced threats from the starving people of Leningrad. Hundreds of thousands of Russians died of hunger in Leningrad during the war. Several of those who died were scientists who protected the large storehouse of seeds.

These scientists protected the seed bank's germplasm collection during the siege of Leningrad for nearly two years. World War II ended in 1945, and the Germans never reached Leningrad. Vavilov's seed bank survived. Following the war, more seed banks were created around the world. Many of these seed banks hold seeds from Vavilov's original collection. Plant breeders have used seeds and germplasm from Vavilov's collection to develop improved varieties of cereals, fruits, and vegetables that feed people worldwide.

As German troops advanced across the Soviet Union during WWII, they captured small seed banks in their path. However, they did not reach the main seed bank in Leningrad.

The work of Vavilov and his fellow scientists created a vast genetic resource for future crops. Their work helped people better understand the importance of biodiversity. They demonstrated how **conserving** germplasm would help ensure **food security** for all people on Earth.

ESSENTIAL QUESTION

Why did humans start cultivating crops in different parts of the world at about the same time?

TEXT TO **WORLD**

Does your family grow a garden? What seeds do you plant? What problems do you sometimes encounter when trying to grow food?

WHAT'S FOR
DINNER?

How is the food we eat today different from the meals prepared by early hunter-gatherer societies? Let's find out! In this activity, you will create a meal that a hunter-gatherer could prepare.

❯ **Research hunting-and-gathering diets.** What were some common foods these societies ate?

❯ **Design a meal that a hunter-gatherer could make.** Consider the following factors.

✱ Where does the hunter-gatherer group live?

✱ What plants and animals are native to that region?

✱ What tools do you need to hunt or gather the food items?

✱ What ingredients do you need? Where can you find each ingredient?

✱ What time of year could you make this meal?

✱ How long would it take to gather enough of these ingredients to feed a family of four? How long would it take to feed a group of 20?

✱ What nutrients does this meal provide?

❯ **Prepare a presentation of the hunter-gatherer meal you designed.** Share it with your family or classmates.

Try This!

What factors would affect whether or not you could prepare this meal? If you can't find some of the ingredients, what could you substitute? Would it be harder or easier to make the new meal? How do these changes affect the meal's nutrition?

Biodiversity Centers

Biodiversity centers ensure that today's crops can survive changing conditions in the future. In biodiversity centers, genes for a wide variety of traits exist. With these genes and traits, scientists can breed crop varieties that resist new pests and diseases or adapt to changing weather and climate.

STICKY SEEDS

Most plants use seeds to reproduce. If plants grow too closely together, they compete for water, soil nutrients, and sunlight. Through a process called seed dispersal, plants spread their seeds to new places. Some seeds are carried to new places by wind and water. Others are spread by animals, either by sticking to their fur or by spreading through their waste after they eat and digest fruit or nuts with seeds. Some seeds grow with hooks and spikes that make it easier to stick to an animal's fur. In this activity, you will design a plant seed that can stick to and be spread by an animal.

❯ **Do some online research.** Look for a few examples of seeds that have hooks and spikes.

❯ **Use the foam ball as the seed's center.** Choose from the various craft materials to design and build a sticky seed.

❯ **To test your sticky seed, put on the wool glove.** Hold your hand parallel to the ground. Attach your sticky seed to the underside of your gloved hand. Does it stick? See how far you can walk with the sticky seed attached to the glove. Mark where it falls off.

❯ **Based on your test, what parts of the seed worked to make it sticky?** What characteristics did not work? Adjust your design and retest the new sticky seed. How does it perform compared to the original design?

❯ **Think about the kind of animals that could carry your sticky seed.** Why would these animals be successful in spreading the seed?

Consider This!

What characteristics made your seed sticky? Do you think these same characteristics would make it good to eat? What type of seed would early farmers have chosen to plant? How would this affect the plant's ability to reproduce? What other methods of seed dispersal do you know about?

WHERE DID YOUR
FOOD ORIGINATE?

TOOL KIT
- printed map of the world
- colored pens or pencils
- paper

Nikolai Vavilov researched crop centers of origin, now called centers of diversity. Through his work, we have a good idea where different foods were first domesticated by early farmers. You can use this information to create a map that shows where the food you eat comes from.

❯ On the world map, mark where you live with a X.

❯ Go through your kitchen and create a list of 10 foods that you commonly eat.

You can use this website for a map and chart of Vavilov's centers of origin.

🔎 Geography Vavilov Origin

❯ Use the internet to research where these foods originated. With a different color for each food, mark the food's center of origin on your map and draw a line from it to your home.

✱ Which foods originated closest to home? Farthest from home?

✱ What would your diet be like if different foods had not spread beyond their centers of origin?

✱ What foods would you have to rely on instead?

What Is Germplasm?

When is a seed not just a seed? When it is part of germplasm! Germplasm is the term used to describe seeds, plant parts, and plants useful for crop research, breeding, and conservation. These plant parts contain genetic material that can be passed on to the plant's offspring. Plants, seeds, or other materials are germplasm when collected and used for studying, managing, or using their genetic information. The seed of a pepper plant in a backyard garden is just a seed. But a pepper seed that was collected to study the genetic diversity of pepper plants or to develop a breeding program for new pepper plants is germplasm.

Chapter 2

MAIZE

In 1493, Italian explorer Christopher Columbus (1451–1506) returned to Europe full of stories and souvenirs from his adventures in the New World. One of the most exciting things he brought was a handful of seeds. In Europe, Columbus had never encountered the grain called maize. It was new, strange, and delicious. He believed that the promising plant could feed many people if Europeans could learn to grow it.

A few hundred years later, Columbus's prediction was on the mark. Today, maize is one of the world's most important crops. Billions of tons of maize are grown on every continent except Antarctica. Maize supplies more than 6 percent of all food calories for people worldwide. Cornbread, tortillas, corn fritters, popcorn, corn chips, and, of course, corn on the cob—all are possible because of maize!

ESSENTIAL QUESTION

Why is growing GMO food controversial?

And we do more than eat maize. Maize feeds **livestock**. It is transformed into **ethanol**, an industrial chemical. It is even used to make plastic. So, how did maize become one of the world's top crops?

AN ANCIENT WILD GRASS

The story of maize begins thousands of years ago in central Mexico. There, an ancient wild grass called teosinte grew. Most scientists believe that teosinte evolved through thousands of years into the tasty maize cobs we love today.

Teosinte looked nothing like modern maize. Maize typically has a tall, single stalk. It produces a long ear that measures up to 12 inches long and holds hundreds of kernels. Teosinte had several smaller shoots that grew ears that measured only 2 to 3 inches long. Each teosinte ear had only 5 to 12 kernels. Teosinte kernels were covered in a hard coating, which allowed them to pass through the digestive tracts of the birds and grazing animals that ate them. The animals then spread the kernel seeds to new areas through their waste, which led to new teosinte plants when conditions were right.

About 9,000 years ago, teosinte grew wild. People living in what is now Mexico began developing it into a crop they could grow. The people noticed that not all teosinte plants were the same. Some plants grew larger than others. Others produced kernels that were easier to grind or tasted better. People saved the kernels—which are seeds—from plants with desirable characteristics. They planted the seeds for the next harvest. This was the first step in domesticating maize. And this process is called artificial selection or **selective breeding**.

Many people think maize is a vegetable, but it is technically a fruit. Fruits are the seed-bearing part of a flowering plant, while vegetables are the edible stems, leaves, and other parts of a plant.

livestock: animals raised for food and other uses.

ethanol: alcohol made from plants that can be used as fuel.

selective breeding: the process of breeding plants or animals for specific traits or combinations of traits—a type of artificial selection.

liquor: an alcoholic drink.

ferment: when a substance breaks down through time into another substance, such as grape juice turning into wine.

DOMESTICATING MAIZE

No one knows precisely how long the domestication of maize took. It most likely happened across thousands of years. And it did not occur in one place. Although domestication may have started in Mexico, maize spread throughout the Americas. Maize spread when groups traded with each other or when people migrated to a new area. As a result, maize evolved in different parts of the Americas.

Across many generations, people continued the selective breeding of maize. They noticed some plants produced exposed kernels, which made the maize easier to eat. Other plants had kernels that remained on the cobs longer, which made them easier to harvest than plants that broke apart and spread individual kernels on the ground. People also probably discovered maize plants that produced more rows of kernels on each ear—meaning more food. This is what people wanted in future crops, so they used the seeds from these plants to grow the next year's harvest.

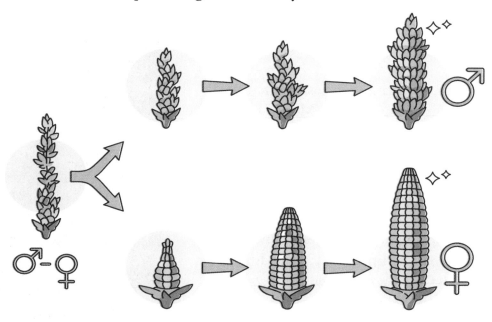

In artificial selection, people keep the seeds from the plants they like best to replant next season to ensure they get those same, desirable characteristics in the next harvest of corn.

Maize's Changing Appearance

Maize today looks much different from how it looked a few thousand years ago. With selective breeding, early farmers picked maize plants with larger kernels, better taste, and higher yields. This process gradually changed the way maize looks. Today, maize ears are larger, with more rows of kernels tightly packed on the cob. The kernels are larger, plumper, and more tender. Maize husks are thinner and easier to remove. Selective breeding also led to many varieties of maize in different colors, shapes, and textures. Kernels can be yellow, white, blue, red, or purple.

Year after year, the process of selective breeding continued. Gradually, the ancient teosinte plants began to change. The kernels started to grow without the hard shell, which made them easier to grind into a powder that people could mix with other ingredients, such as water, and eat. The cobs grew larger and produced more kernels. Eventually, they began to resemble the modern crop we know as maize. Through selective breeding, people turned the wild grass teosinte into maize, a staple food packed with protein and nutrients.

Where does maize grow today? Take a look at this interactive map to find out. What do you notice about the regions that have the greatest yields?

🔎 maize yields graph

A RELIABLE SOURCE OF FOOD

Maize did not become a staple food overnight. Scientists suspect that maize was first used to make an early form of **liquor**. Early maize plants produced cobs and seeds that were too small to be an essential food staple. But the maize stalks produced a sugary juice. Ancient people could have **fermented** the juice to make alcoholic drinks.

THE SCIENCE OF SEEDS

As time passed, selective breeding produced maize plants with larger cobs and more kernels. Slowly, people added maize to their diets, beyond liquor. Scientists have found evidence that some people were eating significant amounts of maize 4,700 years ago. During thousands of years, the consumption of maize steadily increased.

By domesticating maize, people produced a reliable source of food. The nutritious crop was easy to grow, store, and carry. The kernels were ground down into a corn flour that could be used for bread and tortillas. Nomadic tribes began to form more permanent settlements near their maize crops. In time, these settlements became large cities and civilizations, including the Maya, Aztec, and Inca. Maize fed them all.

MAIZE THROUGH THE AMERICAS

Maize spread across the Americas from central Mexico, most likely from seeds carried along trade networks. The crop traveled through Central America and south to South America. It spread north into North America. Along the way, **Indigenous peoples** cultivated maize for their environments, using selective breeding. Varieties of maize evolved to suit the regions where they were grown.

Maize growing in a field

An Ancient Brewery

In 2004, archaeologists discovered the remains of an ancient brewery in southern Peru. The brewery was in the mountaintop city of Cerro Baúl, where members of the Wari Empire lived from 600 to 1000 CE. The Wari brewery made chicha, a fermented drink similar to beer, using local grains such as maize and fruit. In the Wari society, chicha had an important role in rituals and feasts. To make chicha, the Wari boiled the grains, fruit, and other ingredients in water over fire pits. After boiling, the liquid was poured into fermenting jars. After five to seven days, it turned into chicha.

For example, in the southwestern United States, Hopi farmers developed a variety of maize that thrived in the region's high, dry **elevations**. It was suited to the short growing seasons there.

To reach the moisture from melted winter snow below the surface, the Hopi planted their maize deeper than people in other places planted theirs. When the Hopi maize germinated, a single strong root grew downward to find water deep underground. A strong shoot grew upward to the surface. These adaptations to the maize plant helped the Hopi maize survive in the hot, dry environment.

Maize is a nutritious food. It is full of fiber, minerals, and B vitamins, which are good for the brain, eyes, blood, and energy.

In northeastern Maine and in Quebec, Canada, the Mi'kmaq people selectively bred a fast-growing variety of maize called Gaspe. These maize plants had stalks that were 2 feet tall with short, stubby ears ready to harvest 45 days after planting. That was about half the time most maize needed to ripen, making Gaspe one of the fastest-**maturing** varieties of maize. Why would this be an advantage in a northern climate?

THE SCIENCE OF SEEDS

FEEDING MESOAMERICAN CIVILIZATIONS

As time passed, maize became a staple food for people living in Mesoamerica. This is an area that includes the modern countries of northern Costa Rica, Nicaragua, Honduras, El Salvador, Guatemala, Belize, and central to southern Mexico. Maize allowed Mesoamerican civilizations, including the Maya and Aztec, to grow and thrive. These civilizations illustrated the importance of maize in their **myths**, art, and **rituals**.

A Hopi farmer, Lomay Ohungyoma, carries corn stalks on his back around 1887.

The Maya civilization emerged between 7000 **BCE** and 2000 BCE. The Maya people lived in an area of Central America that stretched from northern Belize through Guatemala and into southern Mexico. Maya civilization reached its height between 2000 BCE and 900 AD.

Today, Gaspe is a very rare variety of maize.

During this time, the Maya built cities and pyramids. They established trade networks and improved **irrigation**, water purification, and farming techniques. The Maya were **polytheistic**, which means they believed in many gods. An essential part of the Maya religion was k'uh, the belief that everything, even **inanimate** objects, contained sacredness.

Maya life revolved around maize. Maize was not just something to eat but also a way to explain the world around them. For example, one of the most important Maya gods was Hun Hunahpu, the god of maize. To explain nature's changing seasons, the Maya believed that the maize god is reborn during the growing season and dies after the maize harvest. In this way, the maize god was linked to the cycle of rebirth and the growth of crops.

To honor Hun Hunahpu, the Maya performed rituals. They believed honoring the maize god would ensure a good harvest and protect them from crop-destroying droughts.

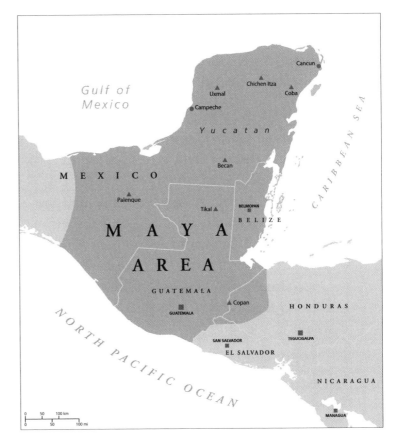

THE SCIENCE OF SEEDS

WORDS TO KNOW

hieroglyphs: a written language that uses pictures and symbols to represent words or ideas.

Several Maya legends feature maize. Maize was central to a Maya creation myth in Popul Vuh, a sacred Maya text. In the tale, the gods first attempted to make humans from clay and wood but failed. Then, the gods formed a dough made from yellow and white maize and used it successfully to form the first humans. The Maya also used images of maize in murals, **hieroglyphs**, and other artifacts.

MAIZE AND THE AZTEC CIVILIZATION

Centuries later, the Aztec civilization flourished in central Mexico between 1300 to 1531. The Aztec were originally a nomadic people. In the early 1300s, they settled on several small islands in Lake Texcoco. In 1325, they founded the city of Tenochtitlan on the site of modern-day Mexico City. Tenochtitlan rivaled the grand cities in Europe in size and magnificence.

Maize also held great importance in Aztec civilization. One of their ancient legends tells how the Aztec obtained maize. In the legend, the Aztec people ate only roots and hunted game animals. Maize was hidden behind the enormous mountains that surrounded their

Maize cobs always have an even number of rows on each ear.

civilization. Many gods tried to part the mountains so the Aztec could reach the maize, but all failed. The Aztec people sent priests to the creator god Quetzalcoatl, who took the form of a feather-covered serpent. The priests asked Quetzalcoatl to help them get maize. The god promised them he would.

While the other gods had failed by using force, Quetzalcoatl tried a more powerful tool: his intelligence. The god transformed himself into a small, black ant and traveled with a red ant toward the mountains. The trip was tough, but Quetzalcoatl overcame each challenge and kept moving forward.

After several days, Quetzalcoatl reached the other side of the mountains and found the maize. Still in his ant form, he picked up a grain of maize between his teeth. He returned to the Aztec people and gave them the grain of maize for planting. Starting with that seed, legend says the Aztec people cultivated and harvested the maize plant. The precious plant fed the Aztec and helped them become strong and create a beautiful civilization.

The average maize plant grows up to 8 feet tall. The world's tallest maize plant reached 48 feet in 2021.

The Aztec worshipped and celebrated different stages in the life cycle of maize with festivals and offerings. They named these stages and illustrated them with images in artwork. Young maize was named Cinteotl and described as a young man. Young fresh maize was also depicted as a young woman named Xilonen. Chicomecoatl represented old maize with dried seeds and was pictured as a woman.

In stone carvings, figures carried maize cobs in their hands. The Aztec believed that making offerings to the gods, creating images, and celebrating the plant's life cycle would ensure a good crop. New plants would grow from the seeds of old plants and give the Aztec people food and life.

unleavened: prepared without using rising agents such as yeast. Unleavened breads are generally flat.

hominy: a food made from ground corn.

hull: the tough outer layer of a grain.

endosperm: the part of a seed that acts as a food store for a developing plant embryo, usually containing starch with protein and other nutrients.

complementary: completing or enhancing by providing something additional.

Three Sisters: the Native American practice of planting corn, squash, and beans together.

fertility: able to produce or reproduce.

NOT YET CORN ON THE COB

Maize had many advantages as a staple crop in the Americas. It could be grown in different places, from wet lowlands to dry mountain regions. Maize provided nutritious food and a source of carbohydrates for energy. And people could use every part of the maize plant. They could weave the husks into baskets or mats or use them to make dolls. They could burn maize cobs as fuel, carve them into darts, or use them to make ceremonial rattling sticks.

Ancient maize was not as easy to eat as modern corn on the cob. Ancient maize required more work to prepare it for eating. People boiled maize, ground it into a paste, and created an **unleavened** dough. They could also use ground maize in maize syrup and maize pudding. They could use dried maize to make **hominy** by soaking the dried corn in a solution of lye or lime. The process removed the maize's **hull** and germ, making it easier to grind, cook, and digest.

A maize deity (Chicomecoatl)
credit: Metropolitan Museum of Art

Popcorn

First popped in the Americas centuries ago, popcorn has become a well-loved food for people worldwide. Popcorn is one of several varieties of maize. Its kernel has a very hard hull that holds a moist, starchy **endosperm**. When heated, the moisture inside the popcorn kernel transforms into steam. Pressure builds in the kernel until it explodes and becomes a fluffy mass. Archaeologists in Peru and Utah have found popcorn kernels that are more than 1,000 years old. In ancient societies, popcorn was eaten as food, scattered in religious ceremonies, and worn as decorations. Popcorn has been eaten as a breakfast food, used to decorate Christmas trees, given as gifts, and enjoyed in movie theaters. Today, Americans eat an estimated 14 billion quarts of popped popcorn each year.

Native Americans spread maize throughout the Americas by way of their extensive trade networks. In the process, people cultivated different varieties of maize. Between rows of maize plants, they planted **complementary** crops such as squash, beans, and melon. You might have heard of this system as the "**Three Sisters**"—we'll learn more about this method later in the book.

Native Americans created many ways to cook, eat, and use maize. They developed strategies to store maize during the winter and keep it safe from pests and mildew.

For Native American societies, maize was more than just food. It held cultural and symbolic meaning. Maize was linked to **fertility** and the cycle of life. It was part of religious rituals and ceremonies. People held maize festivals and harvest ceremonies to celebrate the planting and harvest of maize.

THE SCIENCE OF SEEDS

cornmeal: maize ground into a coarse flour.

cross-pollinated: a plant pollinated by pollen from a different plant.

pollen: a fine, yellow powder produced by flowering plants.

pollination: the process of transferring pollen from the male part of a flower to the female part so that the flower can make seeds.

EUROPEANS ARRIVE

During the late 1400s, Columbus and the Europeans arrived in the Americas. Spanish explorers from that time described a millet-like grain that was popular among the native people. The explorers saw how the Native Americans ground the grain—which was maize—into flour. It was used to make tortillas, maize breads, and mush. The Spanish and Portuguese explorers brought seeds from the maize plants back to their homelands. Maize had arrived in Europe.

By the early 1500s, maize spread from Spain to other parts of Europe, northern Africa, and China. The maize plant easily adapted to new growing environments. For example, maize grew especially successfully in southern and tropical Africa, where there are steady rains and a long growing season.

Maize became a successful crop in countries worldwide. In Europe, maize had a significant impact. It grew well in different environments, which made it valuable, allowing Europeans to depend less on traditional wheat and barley crops. Maize provided a reliable food source for both people and livestock. Because maize helped feed people during food shortages, it made the food supply more stable.

Some varieties of maize grow at sea level, while others grow at altitudes as high as 12,000 feet.

Maize quickly became a staple ingredient in European recipes. It was used in bread, porridge, and stews. Ground maize, called **cornmeal**, became commonly used in European kitchens. Maize was even used in brewing some alcoholic drinks, such as whiskey.

MAIZE SPREADS IN THE UNITED STATES

As Europeans embraced maize, Native Americans taught American colonists how to cultivate it. When the new American farmers spread westward across the vast country, they brought and planted maize seeds. They planted the seeds across the vast country.

Growing plants takes time and patience. But in this video, you can see a maize seed germinate and grow shoots in a time-lapse video! How do plants know which direction to grow?

🔍 green time lapse corn

American farmers continued the practice of selective breeding of maize plants. Farmers saved the seeds from the most desirable plants each fall and planted them the following spring. The plants **cross-pollinated** in the field, which meant that **pollen** released from one plant was carried by the wind over the area and **pollinated** flowers on nearby plants.

THE SCIENCE OF SEEDS

In the middle of the United States, the soil was deep, rich, and fertile. The land was mostly flat. Hot days, warm nights, and enough rain created ideal conditions for growing maize and other crops. Maize became the area's main crop. The region was soon known as the "Corn Belt." The Corn Belt stretched across the midwestern states of Illinois, Indiana, Iowa, Michigan, Minnesota, Missouri, Ohio, and Wisconsin.

Because of its high sugar content, corn can be turned into a syrup.

Maize became an important part of American farm life. Around the 1900s, maize competitions became a popular social event in the Corn Belt. At county and state fairs in the fall, farmers entered 10-ear samples of maize for judging. Judges evaluated the maize for the **uniform** appearance of ears and kernels and awarded prizes to the winners. As a result, growing maize with uniform size and appearance became even more important to many farmers during the early 1900s.

CREATING HYBRID VIGOR

In the United States, two scientists named Edward East (1879–1938) and George Shull (1874–1954) began experimenting with the pollination of maize plants. Most of the time, a field of maize plants is cross-pollinated, which means one plant is pollinated by pollen from nearby plants. East and Shull experimented with the **self-pollination** of maize plants. In self-pollination, a plant is pollinated by pollen from itself.

East and Shull made an interesting discovery. They learned that self-pollinated maize plants produced offspring more similar to the parent plants than cross-pollinated plants. They continued to self-pollinate the offspring plants. Each time, the offspring had fewer differences from the parent plant. After the process was repeated about seven times, a plant called an **inbred** was produced. An inbred is a pure-breeding strain of maize. If the inbred plant is self-pollinated, all of its offspring will be genetically identical to the parent and each other.

> Did you know there are five main types of corn? Flint, flour, dent, sweet, and popcorn! Use this chart to learn more about each type. Which kinds are you most familiar with?
>
>
>
> 𝒫 Native Seeds corn type

This process created maize plants and the cobs they produced that were uniform and consistent. But inbred maize had a problem. The plants lost **vigor**. They were not as healthy and did not grow as well or produce as much food. Scientists, however, found a way to solve this problem. When they crossed two inbred maize plants, the offspring was a **hybrid** plant that grew larger and produced more maize. This concept became known as **hybrid vigor**. Today, most commercial maize grown in the United States is hybrid.

Pollination

Many plants reproduce through a process called pollination. In most plants, a flower has both male and female parts. The male part is a **stamen**, and it produces a powdery substance called pollen. Pollination is the process of moving pollen from the stamen to another plant's female part, called a **pistil**. When insects sit on a plant's flowers to sip a sweet fluid called **nectar**, grains of pollen stick to them. When the insect flies to the next flower, it transfers the pollen. Sometimes, the wind carries pollen from one plant to another. When pollen reaches the pistil, fertilization occurs, and the plant produces fruit or seeds. Take a look at page vi to learn more!

THE SCIENCE OF SEEDS

WORDS TO KNOW

open-pollinate: when plants are pollinated by bees, moths, birds, bats, and other natural methods.

innovation: a new creation or a unique solution to a problem.

till: to turn the soil to control for weeds and pests and to prepare for seeding.

herbicide: a chemical used to kill unwanted plants such as weeds.

crop rotation: the practice of growing a series of different types of crops in the same area across a sequence of growing seasons to restore the soil's nutrients.

genetic engineering: the process of manipulating genes to alter the appearance and other characteristics of an organism.

genome: an organism's complete set of genetic material.

genetically modified organism (GMO): an organism whose DNA has been modified.

mechanization: the use of machines to perform work.

climate change: a change in long-term weather patterns, which can happen through natural or manmade processes.

GROWING MORE MAIZE

Before the 1930s, American farmers grew **open-pollinated** maize varieties, which meant they were pollinated only by insects and other things in nature. Between 1866 and 1936, the yields of open-pollinated maize remained relatively stable. American farmers often produced an average of 25 bushels per acre every year.

During the late 1930s, farmers rapidly adopted the new hybrid maize varieties. These plants produced a lot more food. Within a few years, maize yields began to increase dramatically. Between 1937 and 1955, maize yield increased nearly a bushel per acre yearly. Farmers were likely amazed by this rapid increase!

Other farming **innovations** also helped to increase maize yields. Widespread use of fertilizers made most land that could be **tilled** suitable for planting maize. Fertilizers give crops nutrients, such as nitrogen, potassium, and phosphorus, which allow the crops to grow bigger and produce more food. Nitrogen, in particular, is an essential nutrient for the growth of all living organisms.

Effective **herbicides** allowed farmers to remove weeds from maize fields more easily. This gave maize plants the space to grow bigger and produce more food. Pesticides protected the maize plants from disease and pests.

Weeds can be managed naturally by hand pulling, mulching to smother the weeds, and crop rotation.

GMO Maize

During the 1990s, scientists discovered how to use **genetic engineering** to change an organism's **genome**. This process genetically alters an organism to change its characteristics and results in a **genetically modified organism (GMO)**. Today, most of the maize grown in the United States is a GMO variety. GMO maize varieties were primarily designed to be pest-resistant and herbicide-tolerant. Also, researchers have discovered they can increase maize yield by up to 10 percent by changing a gene that controls plant growth. However, there is some controversy surrounding GMO food crops, as the long-term effects on human health are unknown.

Mechanization also had a significant impact on maize yields. For generations, cultivating maize was labor-intensive. Early crops had to be harvested by hand. It took about 20 hours of labor to produce a single bushel of maize! Farmers planted maize seeds by hand in tilled earth. With mechanical tools, farmers did not have to cultivate maize entirely by hand. Machinery such as tractors, planters, and pickers allowed farmers to plant more maize and harvest it more quickly. As a result, maize yields increased even more.

Take a look at how this Illinois family harvests maize on their family farm. How is this different from 100 years ago? What does that mean for the crops?

Illinois Farm Families #360 corn

MODERN MAIZE CULTIVATION

Today, modern U.S. farmers can plant entire fields of maize with a single commercial hybrid variety. Seed companies develop maize varieties that have precisely controlled traits. Commercial seeds are bred to resist disease and **climate change**. They are also bred for other characteristics that produce a consistent harvest.

TEXT TO **WORLD**

What is your favorite form of maize? Cornbread? Tortillas? Popcorn?

THE SCIENCE OF SEEDS

WORDS TO KNOW

technology: the tools, methods, and systems used to solve a problem or do work.

autonomous: without human contact.

In addition, modern U.S. maize farmers use precision agriculture **technologies** such as global positioning (GPS) technology, drone and satellite images, and **autonomous** machines to monitor maize crops closely. These technologies provide detailed information about crop growth, health, and yield. They also allow farmers to protect crops from pests, disease, and climate risks more efficiently than ever.

Because of these innovations, the United States is the world's largest producer of maize. In 2021, U.S. farmers produced 15.1 billion bushels of maize, an increase of 7 percent from 2020, according to the U.S. Department of Agriculture (USDA). And throughout the world, farmers are producing more maize today than at any other point in history.

Maize is an important crop for humans, both now, in the past, and in the future. In the next chapter, we'll take a look at another seed with a long history—wheat!

ESSENTIAL QUESTION

Why is growing GMO food controversial?

WRITE A
MAIZE MYTH

In many civilizations, myths are sacred tales that explain the surrounding world and how it works. Myths answer questions and explain how natural events occurred. They are often used to explain the creation of life and Earth. Myths can also teach lessons and values. Traditional myths are passed down from generation to generation through oral storytelling. In this activity, you will use your creativity to write a maize myth.

❯ **Brainstorm some ideas for your myth.** What part of the story of maize do you want to tell? For example, you could write a story about the origin of maize or about how maize grows, the maize harvest, or maize as food.

❯ **Once you have a myth idea, think about the following elements:**

✳ Characters

✳ Setting

✳ Plot

✳ Moral or main idea

❯ **After you have decided these details, get started writing.** After you have finished, share your myth with your family or class. See if they get the moral or main idea from the myth.

Try This!

Using the myth you wrote above, create a comic strip that tells the same story.

The Three Sisters

Indigenous people in the Americas often planted three crops together: maize, beans, and squash. Together, these plants were known as the Three Sisters. According to legend, the three plants were a gift from the gods and were always to be grown, eaten, and celebrated together. Maize provided support for the beans to grow and wrap around. The beans added nitrogen to the soil, which acted as a natural fertilizer. Squash was usually planted between the corn and beans. Its large leaves blocked heat from the sun and helped the soil stay moist.

NIXTAMALIZATION
OF MAIZE

First used by the people of Mesoamerica, **nixtamalization** is the process of soaking dried maize in a solution to soften the kernel and improve its taste. The alkaline solution was traditionally made from wood ashes mixed with water. Nixtamalization made maize kernels easier to cook. It also made them more nutrient-rich and added calcium and niacin, two essential minerals for the human body. Without nixtamalization, many people who rely on maize for food would be at risk of nutrient deficiencies. In this activity, you will learn how to nixtamalize corn.

TOOL KIT
- dried corn (dent corn, field corn, or even popcorn kernels)
- pickling lime or baking soda
- cooking pot and lid
- measuring cup
- tablespoon
- strainer

> **Ask an adult to help with the stove!**

> **Put 2 cups of dried corn into a cooking pot.** Add 2 quarts (8 cups) of water and 1 tablespoon of pickling lime or baking soda.

> **Bring the water to a boil.** Reduce heat and simmer uncovered for 30 minutes, stirring occasionally. After 30 minutes, turn off the heat, cover the pot with a lid, and put it aside to sit overnight.

> **The next morning, take a look inside the pot.** What do the kernels look like? How have they changed?

> **Place the corn in a bowl under running water.** Rub the kernels through your hands to loosen the skins from the kernels. Put the bare kernels in a strainer and rinse thoroughly. Store in an airtight container in the refrigerator. It will keep for a few days. You can grind the nixtamalized corn into a dough called masa for tortillas or tamales— try this in the next activity!

Consider This!

Why do you think people living in more permanent settlements were more likely to rely on maize as a food source? Why would it be difficult for a nomadic community to rely on maize? Would nixtamalization be easier for one community? Why?

WORDS TO KNOW

nixtamalization: to soak dried maize in a solution to soften the kernel and improve its taste.

MAKE
MASA DOUGH

TOOL KIT

- 2 cups of nixtamalized maize (from previous activity)
- food processor
- ½ teaspoon salt
- ¼ cup water

Masa is a maize dough that is made from ground, nixtamalized maize. Masa is used to make corn tortillas, tamales, and many other Mexican and Latin American foods.

Ask an adult to help with the stove!

❯ **Measure out the nixtamalized maize, salt, and water.** Combine them in a food processor.

❯ **Blend and pulse the processor to grind the maize.** You may have to stop a few times to scrape the sides. If more moisture is needed, add water 1 tablespoon at a time.

❯ **After about 4 to 5 minutes, the maize mixture will form a thick, doughy substance.**

Masa can be fermented, wrapped **in corn husks, and steamed to make** kenkey, a West African staple food.

❯ **Take a golf ball-sized piece of the dough and pat it into a flat circle, as thin as you can make it.** If the dough is too wet to handle, let it dry out a bit first.

❯ **Heat a frying pan or griddle to medium heat.** Place the dough on the griddle and cook for about 45 to 60 seconds on each side. Place the cooked tortilla on a plate and enjoy!

❯ **Any masa dough that is not used immediately can be covered and stored in the refrigerator.** It will keep for a few days.

Consider This!

What else could you make with masa dough? Are there other foods that would complement masa? What nutrition would it provide?

THE THREE SISTERS:
COMPLETE NUTRITION

The Three Sisters not only grow better together, they also provide better nutrition when eaten together. Let's find out how by making a Three Sisters dish—succotash!

Ask an adult to help with the stove!

❯ **Research each food—maize, beans, and squash.** What nutrients does each one provide that are essential for humans?

❯ **What is special about eating these three foods together?** What nutritional benefit do they provide together that they do not provide individually? How is this helpful when meat is scarce or if someone chooses not to eat meat?

❯ **Now, try your hand at making a Three Sisters dish—succotash.** In a large skillet, heat the butter over medium heat until melted.

❯ **Add the onion and saute about 5 minutes.** When the onion starts to look clear on the edges, add the chopped zucchini. After the zucchini has cooked for about 5 minutes, add the cut corn and lima beans.

❯ **Heat through, about 2 minutes.** Remove from the heat and add salt and pepper to taste. Serve and enjoy!

Consider This!

What other recipes can you make using the Three Sisters?

Corn Pollination

With corn, the stamens are found in the tassels that appear at the top of each stalk of corn. The pistils are in the silky threads that grow from each potential kernel. If the pollen from the tassels reaches the silken threads, the kernel is fertilized and can begin to develop into mature corn.

Chapter 3

WHEAT

What would bread taste like without wheat? Imagine making donuts, cookies, crackers, cakes, pizza, and tortillas without wheat. Some beer is even made with wheat! Wheat is one of the world's most important crops. Without wheat, many foods we eat would not taste the same.

In 2021, more than 776 million metric tons of wheat were produced. An elephant often weighs just one metric ton. Imagine 776 million elephants! Wheat was the world's second-most produced grain behind maize. Two-thirds of the wheat grown feeds people worldwide. For many people, wheat is an essential part of their diet. Wheat provides protein, carbohydrates, vitamins, and minerals.

ESSENTIAL QUESTION

Why is it important for farmers to stay informed about the science of the crops they are planting?

Wheat is more than human food. Wheat is used in animal feed, particularly for poultry and livestock. Wheat is also used in **biofuels**, paper production, and construction materials. So, how did the world come to rely on wheat?

THE SCIENCE OF SEEDS

WORDS TO KNOW

biofuel: a fuel made from living matter, such as plants.

organic: something that is or was living, such as animals, wood, grass, and insects. Also refers to food grown naturally, without chemicals.

ORIGINS OF WHEAT

The story of wheat goes back about 10,000 years to a region known as the Fertile Crescent. This area was a crescent-shaped region in the Middle East. It includes modern Iraq, Turkey, Syria, Lebanon, Israel, Palestine, and Egypt. Much of the area was bordered by mountains on one side and desert on the other. See page 16 for a map.

The Fertile Crescent got its name from its shape and rich soils. The nearby Tigris and Euphrates Rivers regularly overflowed their banks during the rainy seasons. River water flooded the land. The river water carried sand, silt, and debris full of **organic** matter and minerals. When the floodwaters receded, the materials remained and created an area of fertile soil in the dry, sandy region. The fertile soil was ideal for growing strong and healthy plants because it provided plenty of the nutrients the plants needed.

Milling wheat to make flour is a multi-step process. Take a look at this diagram to see how it is done. How can one type of wheat be processed differently to make several different types of flour?

🔍 wheat foods milled

PS

Hunter-gatherers living in the Fertile Crescent gathered the wild grasses that grew in the fertile soil, including two ancient wheat varieties, emmer and einkorn. At first, early humans probably ate their wheat grains raw. In time, they learned to use stone tools to crack and pound the tough grains. They could mix the cracked grains with water to create a porridge-like food. Left in the sun, the grain mixture formed a dry, bread-like crust. Sound appetizing? Early diets were much different from ours!

50

CULTIVATION IN ABU HUREYRA

Sometime between about 11,500 and 7,000 years ago, a group of hunter-gatherers formed the Abu Hureyra village in the valley of the Euphrates River. As generations passed, the Abu Hureyra people gradually transitioned from hunting and gathering to farming.

In the remains of this ancient village, archaeologists have uncovered some of the earliest evidence of wheat cultivation in the Fertile Crescent. They found evidence of stone tools, mortars, grinding stones, and pottery. Scientists believe these tools were used for cultivating ancient wheat.

The ancient wheat species that grew in the region, emmer and einkorn, had grains covered with a hard hull coating. In the wild, tough hulls protected the wheat grains from predators. But for ancient people, the hulls made the wheat challenging to eat. To make the wheat grains usable, people had to pound the seeds to break off the hulls and release the grains. They could then grind the grains into flour, which could be used to make food.

Emmer wheat

THE SCIENCE OF SEEDS

Grinding wheat grains took a lot of time and energy. Most of the grinding was done by the village women.

Archaeologists have studied bones found at the Abu Hureyra site for clues about how they lived. The women's bones showed signs of spending many hours kneeling to grind wheat grains. Hours of grinding may have produced just enough flour for a single meal.

As difficult as wheat grains were to grind, they were easy to store. And the wheat gave the people a reliable source of food that lasted for months. As Abu Hureyra slowly adopted farming, its population grew. The village became one of the largest settlements in the Middle East.

George Washington had a gristmill on his property at Mount Vernon, Virginia. You can watch a video of the gristmill in operation here. How does this video show the connection between food and engineering?

🔍 Mount Vernon gristmill

Grinding stones from the Abu Hureyra village
credit: Zunkir (CC BY SA 4.0)

DOMESTICATING WHEAT

As people first domesticated wheat, they selected plants with favorable characteristics, just as people did with maize. The rachis is a stem that keeps the wheat shafts together in wheat plants. When wild wheat is ripe, the rachis shatters, and its seeds spread on the ground.

People probably found it difficult and time-consuming to gather seeds that were scattered on the ground. In time, they selected plants that held their seeds longer or did not drop them at all.

One bushel of wheat can make 90 one-pound loaves of whole wheat bread.

Early farmers also chose wheat plants with softer hulls. A softer hull made wheat grains easier to grind and process for food. They picked plants that produced the largest grains. As many seasons passed, farmers also selected plants that grew taller than weeds, which made it easier to grow and harvest the wheat.

Gluten Intolerance

As people ate more wheat, some discovered it did not agree with them. Wheat contains a protein called **gluten**. Gluten gives bread its chewy texture. Some people have celiac disease, which causes an **autoimmune** response to gluten. Their bodies try to fight gluten, which causes inflammation and damage to the digestive system. Other people have a gluten intolerance. Eating gluten makes them feel sick, bloated, gassy, or tired. Today, people with celiac disease or a gluten intolerance can choose gluten-free foods. These foods do not contain wheat or other grains with gluten. Does anyone in your family eat only gluten-free foods?

It is unknown how long it took people to domesticate wheat. Some scientists believe it occurred rapidly during just a few centuries. Others believe that domestication of wheat took much longer, up to 5,000 years.

THE SCIENCE OF SEEDS

WORDS TO KNOW

cuneiform: a system of wedge-shaped letters created by ancient civilizations.

sickle: a sharp farming tool in the shape of a half moon used for cutting grain.

thresh: to separate wheat grains from the rest of the plant.

ANCIENT CIVILIZATIONS IN THE FERTILE CRESCENT

Agriculture and the domestication of wheat allowed civilizations to grow in the Fertile Crescent. Sumer, one of the earliest known civilizations, was settled around 4500 to 4000 BCE. Sumer was located between the Tigris and Euphrates Rivers in a region that is modern southern Iraq. The Sumerians are known for several inventions, including the world's first writing system, called **cuneiform**.

The Sumerians wrote about their lives on clay tablets. They recorded poems and creation myths. One creation myth was called "The Debate between Grain and Sheep." The myth was written on clay tablets sometime between 3000 and 2000 BCE.

The myth tells the story of the Sumerian god An, who created Ashnan, the goddess of grain, and Lahar, the sheep goddess. In the myth, the two goddesses helped humans learn how to plant grain and raise sheep.

Sumerian cuneiform clay tablet

Then, the two goddesses argued over who was more important to humans. Eventually, the god of wisdom declared Ashnan the winner. He reasoned that grain was more important because grain does not need sheep to live, but sheep cannot live without grain. Many people worshipped Ashnan throughout Sumer and prayed to her for successful plantings and harvests.

BREAD IN ANCIENT EGYPT

From the Fertile Crescent, wheat spread into Europe, Africa, and Asia between 2000 and 500 BCE. In Ancient Egypt, people embraced wheat. It became one of their staple foods. The Ancient Egyptians used a handheld tool called a **sickle** to harvest wheat. They stacked the cut wheat and used oxen to **thresh** it by stomping on it. Threshing is separating wheat grains from the rest of the plant.

With emmer wheat and barley, the Egyptians made bread. Bread made from wheat was an essential source of protein, vitamins, and minerals. It quickly became part of every meal. Ancient Egyptians of all backgrounds, from workers to kings, ate bread.

The average North American eats about 53 pounds of bread every year.

At first, the Ancient Egyptians made simple bread by mixing flour from ground wheat with water and salt.

The Egyptians made the mixture into a flat circle and put it on a hot rock next to the fire to cook. The result was a flatbread that looked like today's pita bread. Through time, the Egyptians formed more intricate shapes with the bread dough.

Bread Wheat

About 8,000 years ago, a new species of wheat appeared in the wild. The new species was created when the pollen of a goatgrass species fertilized an emmer plant. This occurred naturally, without human help. The new wheat variety was called bread wheat. It had a softer hull that could be more easily removed. Bread wheat also had a softer seed, which was much easier to grind into flour. When ground into flour, bread wheat made light and airy dough. People quickly favored this variety!

THE SCIENCE OF SEEDS

At some point, the Egyptians learned how to make yeast-**leavened** bread. Without yeast or other leavening agents, bread made from wheat was flat and dense. We don't know how the first yeast-leavened bread was made. It may have even happened by accident! Perhaps some yeast landed on dough that had been left out. Or maybe some ale with yeast was mixed with the ground flour instead of water. Or wild yeast floating in the air may have gotten into the dough.

No matter how it happened, yeast causes a chemical reaction with the starch in the wheat flour. The reaction releases **carbon dioxide** gas bubbles that puff up the bread, giving it a light and fluffy texture.

Egyptian bakers would shape the yeasty dough in various molds and allow it to rise. Then, they baked the bread in ovens made from mud and bricks.

Workers who built the Egyptian pyramids were fed a daily ration of about 10 loaves of bread.

A Kernel of Wheat

The wheat kernel grows in the head of the wheat plant. Each kernel has three main parts: endosperm, **bran**, and **germ**. The endosperm provides nutrients and energy to the germ so it can grow and develop into a new plant. Bran is the kernel's hard, outer covering. The germ is the tiny part of the kernel that sprouts and grows into a new wheat plant. During milling, the three parts of the kernel are separated. White flour is made from just the endosperm. Whole meal flour is made from the entire kernel and is healthier for you.

Follow this link to look at a diagram of a wheat kernel and learn a little more about each part.

🔎 Wheat Foods kernel

An Egyptian statue of a woman grinding wheat, around 2420–2323 BCE

Although the Egyptians were the first to make yeast-leavened bread, they did not fully understand what caused it to rise. It was not until the 1800s that scientists identified yeast and the chemical process that produced carbon dioxide gas. Wheat is the only grain with enough gluten starch for the process to work well. It quickly became the favored grain for bread-making over other grains such as oats, rice, barley, and millet. But bakers add these other grains to bread along with wheat to make delicious flavors!

Bread loaves were a common part of Egyptian burials and provided the dead with food on the journey to the afterlife. Some tombs included model granaries that held wheat and other grains.

landrace: a locally adapted variety of a species.

reap: to cut or gather a crop or harvest.

manure: animal waste.

immigrant: a person who comes to live in another country.

WHEAT SPREADS TO NEW AREAS

Slowly, wheat spread from the Fertile Crescent to new regions in Africa, Europe, and Asia. It traveled on trade routes and moved as people migrated to new areas. The people in these areas selected wheat plants that adapted best to the local environment and climate. Through time, new **landraces** of wheat emerged. A landrace is a domesticated and locally adapted variety of a species. The landraces of wheat developed traits that helped them survive and thrive in their new environments.

As people migrated to new areas, they also brought their agricultural practices. They sowed, **reaped**, and threshed wheat plants. They ground wheat flour. And they baked wheat bread. They learned to feed wheat grain to domesticated cattle to produce meat and milk. The cattle produced **manure** that could be used to fertilize the wheat fields.

Hori, an ancient Egyptian high priest, sitting at a table with three different kinds of bread and a variety of vegetables and meat

When Christopher Columbus and other European explorers arrived in the New World, they brought wheat. Wheat cultivation spread from Mexico during the early 1500s to the southwestern United States.

Other explorers brought grains of wheat to North America's east coast. American colonists, including a farmer named George Washington (1732–1799), grew wheat as one of their crops.

The western Mississippi Valley and the Great Plains of the United States provided large areas of fertile land for wheat farming. During the 1870s, American farmers discovered that the Turkey Red wheat, a hard red winter wheat variety, grew well in the region. This variety, introduced to the Kansas farmlands by Russian Mennonite **immigrants**, spread quickly across American farmland.

IMPROVEMENTS IN FARMING

For thousands of years, there were few advances in wheat farming. Cultivating wheat was a very labor-intensive process. Farmers relied on human workers and domesticated horses and oxen to plant, harvest, and process wheat. As a result, farmers were limited in how much wheat they could cultivate.

THE SCIENCE OF SEEDS

WORDS TO KNOW

deplete: to use up, drain, or empty.

Industrial Revolution: a period during the eighteenth and nineteenth centuries when large cities and factories began to replace small towns and farming.

scythe: a tool that consists of a long, curved blade on a pole with two handles that is used for cutting grain crops.

export: to send goods to another country to sell.

dormant: to be in a resting and inactive state.

The land also limited what farmers could do. Planting wheat crops year after year on the same fields **depleted** nutrients in the soil. Without essential soil nutrients, wheat did not grow as well. Farmers often had to leave some fields unplanted for a season to restore the soil's nutrients. They might also practice crop rotation and plant a different crop on that field. Farmers also needed some fields to grow hay instead of wheat. They fed their horses, oxen, and other work animals the hay.

During the **Industrial Revolution** in the 1800s, new machines, such as the mechanical reaper, mechanical thresher, and steel plow, all made farming more efficient. With these machines, farmers could plant more wheat and they could harvest it much faster. With a mechanical reaper, a farmer could harvest five to six acres daily compared to one acre with a handheld **scythe**.

A farmer using an early mechanical reaper

Once harvested, the wheat could be threshed much faster as well. Using a mechanical thresher, farmers could process wheat grain about 30 times faster than they could by hand. A new type of mill that used steel rollers powered by steam engines made it easier to mill wheat into flour.

Cross-country railroads improved the delivery of wheat, taking it from farms to people throughout the country. Between 1866 and 1900, U.S. wheat production grew from 175 million bushels to 655 million bushels. American farmers were now producing more than enough wheat to feed the country. They could start **exporting** it to other countries worldwide.

Today, the United States is one of the world's largest wheat exporters, along with Russia, Canada, France, and Ukraine.

During the early 1900s, many U.S. farmers still used horses or mules to pull machines to plow soil, plant seeds, and harvest wheat crops. The development of the gasoline-powered tractor was another significant farming improvement. By 1930, many wheat farmers had swapped their horses for tractors. With tractors, farmers needed fewer workers to plow, plant, and harvest the same number of acres.

Categories of Wheat

Today, six main categories of wheat are grown around the world.

Hard wheat categories include hard red winter, hard red spring, durum, and hard white. Hard wheat varieties typically have higher amounts of protein than soft wheat. The higher protein levels make these varieties better for making bread, buns, pasta, pizza crusts, and other bread products.

Soft wheat categories include soft red winter and soft white wheat. Soft wheat has less protein than hard wheat, making it best for making softer cookies, pastries, crackers, and Asian noodles.

Spring wheat is planted in the spring and is ready for harvest in the summer. Winter wheat is planted in the fall and grows several inches before going **dormant** for the winter. Then, it grows in the spring and is harvested in the summer. In places such as China, a few spring wheat varieties are planted in the fall.

WORDS TO KNOW

famine: a severe shortage of food resulting in widespread hunger.

poverty: without enough income for the basic needs for living.

Green Revolution: a time during the twentieth century when changes in agricultural practices resulted in more food being produced.

THE GREEN REVOLUTION AND WHEAT

During the 1900s, wheat farmers in various countries, including Mexico, struggled with depleted soil and poor wheat crop yields. At the same time, the world's population was growing rapidly. Some people predicted the world's crops could not keep up with the growing population. If the world could not produce enough food to feed everyone, millions would face food shortages and **famine**.

To prevent these scary predictions from happening, scientists wanted to find a way to increase the production of essential crops, including wheat and rice. During the 1940s, an American scientist named Norman Borlaug (1914–2009) teamed up with Mexican scientists to develop a new hybrid wheat variety. They wanted to create a wheat variety that resisted disease and produced higher yields.

Gristmills

The first gristmills in the Americas were built during the 1600s. By the 1800s, many towns had a gristmill to grind wheat and other grains. Gristmills were built next to a fast river. They used the river's current to turn a water wheel, which turned heavy stones that ground wheat into flour or corn into cornmeal. People could buy sacks of flour or cornmeal from the town's general store. Today, most gristmills have been replaced by large modern grain mills.

Borlaug and his team developed a smaller, fast-growing wheat variety using selective breeding. The new wheat variety used soil nutrients more efficiently. It had shorter stems that could better support the weight of heavier ears of grain. It could also grow in any season, which meant farmers could cultivate more wheat each year.

In 1970, Borlaug won the Nobel Peace Prize for his work. The citation read, "More than any other person of this age, he helped provide bread for a hungry world."

The impact of Borlaug's wheat was significant. By the mid-1960s, Mexico produced enough wheat to feed its entire population. Scientists used Borlaug's techniques on other crops to help other countries struggling with food insecurity. During the 1960s, India and Pakistan were also experiencing increased populations and food shortages. They adopted the Mexican wheat program and found that the new wheat varieties grew well in their countries. Wheat production increased significantly by 1970.

Between the 1960s and the 1990s, adopting the new hybrid wheat varieties led to doubling wheat crop yields in Asia. New irrigation techniques, pesticides, and fertilizers also improved yields. Because there was so much wheat available, the price of grain fell. People ate more, and **poverty** rates dropped.

Although the **Green Revolution** helped feed the world, it had drawbacks. Selective breeding for traits that would result in high yields meant that other traits were lost. Genes that made plants more nutritious or better able to resist certain pests or diseases were passed over to make plants that produced a lot of food. Farmers stopped cultivating more diverse local wheat varieties. Increasingly, they cultivated a few new, high-yield hybrid varieties. Genetic diversity declined. And the risk to crops from a new pest, disease, or natural event rose.

ESSENTIAL QUESTION

Why is it important for farmers to stay informed about the science of the crops they are planting?

Now, let's take a look at another crop that you probably have in your pantry—rice!

MAKE
FLOUR TORTILLAS

Wheat is a staple food for people worldwide. Many use wheat to make bread, cakes, pastries, bagels, muffins, tortillas, and more. In this activity, you will use wheat flour to make tortillas that you can eat!

❯ **Place flour, salt, and baking powder in a mixing bowl.** Stir a few times to mix.

❯ **Add shortening to the mixture.** Rub the shortening and flour mixture between your fingers until no large pieces of shortening are left and the mixture looks crumbly.

❯ **Add the hot water to the bowl.** Knead the dough with your hands until the sides of the bowl are clean and the dough is formed into one large ball.

❯ **Spread a piece of wax paper on a table or counter.** Divide the dough into four equal pieces and place them on the wax paper. Cover the dough with a second piece of wax paper and let it rest for about 20 minutes.

❯ **After resting, pat the dough into 8- to 10-inch circles, as flat as you can make them.** If the dough is sticky, sprinkle a little more flour on it.

❯ **Heat a frying pan or griddle to medium heat.** Place the dough on the griddle and cook until dark brown spots appear on the bottom side. Flip and cook the other side until brown. Place the cooked tortilla on a plate. It is ready to eat! Cook the remaining three tortillas the same way.

Consider This!

Do you prefer flour or corn tortillas? Compare the wheat flour tortillas to the masa dough and tortillas from an earlier activity. What differences did you observe? Which was easier to make?

TEXT TO **WORLD**

What kind of bread is your favorite? Do you prefer white or whole grain bread? Does the nutritional value of your bread make a difference to you?

GROW YOUR OWN
WHEATGRASS

TOOL KIT
- wheat kernels from a grocery or gardening store
- strainer
- medium-sized glass jar
- cheesecloth
- elastic band

Farmers worldwide grow millions of acres of wheat. Now, it's your turn! In this activity, you will grow wheatgrass in a jar. Wheatgrass is the first sprouts of the wheat plant. It's used in food and drinks and can be eaten fresh or freeze-dried for later.

❯ Place some wheat kernels in a strainer. Rinse completely with water.

❯ Pour the rinsed kernels into a glass jar and cover with water. Leave the kernels to soak overnight.

❯ The next day, drain the water, rinse the wheat kernels, and return them to the glass jar. This time, cover the jar opening with cheesecloth. Secure the cheesecloth to the jar with an elastic band. Gently place the jar on its side in a dark place and leave overnight again.

❯ Every morning, rinse and drain the wheat kernels. Return them to the jar, cover with cheesecloth, and lay the jar on its side in a dark place. Repeat this process until the kernels sprout.

❯ When the sprouts measure about 1 inch, put the jar in a sunny window for 24 hours. You can now harvest the wheatgrass and enjoy in a salad, sandwich, or a wheatgrass smoothie.

Consider This!

What are the health benefits of adding wheatgrass to your diet?

Chapter 4

RICE

What is your favorite rice recipe? Sushi, paella, fried rice, and risotto are just a few of the delicious foods made with rice in homes and restaurants across the globe. Rice can be part of the main meal, served as a side dish, featured in soups and appetizers, and even be part of dessert.

Rice is grown on every continent on Earth except Antarctica. Worldwide, 3.5 billion people rely on rice as a food staple. That is nearly half of the people on the planet! Each tiny grain of rice is an excellent source of carbohydrates, which supply quick energy to the human body. How did this grain become such an essential part of the human diet? Why do so many people eat rice?

Like wheat and maize, the modern rice plant began life as a wild grain. Wild rice provided early humans with an energy-dense food source. Nearly 10,000 years ago, in southern China, people gathered wild rice.

ESSENTIAL QUESTION

Why is it important for new varieties of rice to be both tasty and healthy?

Archaeologists have found evidence of stone tools from that period used to harvest wild rice grains in ancient villages in China's Lower Yangtze River Valley.

The wild rice plant shattered when ripe, and its seeds fell to the ground. If conditions were good with enough warmth and rain, some seeds germinated and grew into new plants. Shedding seeds was an essential part of the life cycle for wild rice plants. If the plants did not drop their seeds on the ground, new plants could not grow.

The average American eats 27 pounds of rice annually.

Then, about 8,000 years ago, a rare **mutation** occurred in the wild rice plant. A single gene mutation caused the plant to keep its seeds on the stalk. This mutation would have been disastrous for wild rice because it would have been very difficult for the plants to produce offspring. But for the people harvesting rice grains, this worked out well. Instead of gathering tiny grains of rice from the ground, they could harvest rice while it was still on the stalk. People favored seeds from plants with this mutation to plant for future harvests.

THE SCIENCE OF SEEDS

WORDS TO KNOW

mutation: a change in an organism's genes.

anthocyanins: blue, violet, or red bitter-flavored pigments in plants.

awn: a stiff, bristle-like part attached to a plant.

paddy field: a flat field that floods with water and can be used to grow rice.

terrace: a level area cut into a steep slope to provide a flat section to plant crops.

erosion: the gradual wearing away of soil by water or wind.

Wild rice plants sprouted at different times of the year, which protected the plant's survival. If a strong wind or heat wave destroyed vulnerable plants, a new group of seeds was ready to sprout later. However, for farmers, this trait was not ideal. It was easier to harvest all the plants at the same time. Therefore, people probably selected seeds that germinated immediately after sowing for future crops. As a result, the seeds of domesticated rice today typically sprout immediately after planting. That's artificial selection in action!

Early farmers also selected rice seeds for appearance and taste. Wild rice contained bitter pigments called **anthocyanins**. Anthocyanins served an important purpose. Their bitter taste protected wild rice grains from pests and other enemies. But they did not taste great. When a mutation led to a rice plant without anthocyanins, early farmers liked it much more.

Wild rice has a long kernel with a bristle-like **awn** at the top. The awn is part of the wild plant's defenses. It makes the grain hard for animals to swallow and eat. While this trait benefits wild rice, early farmers preferred plants with a shorter grain and a barbless awn, which made it easier to harvest, handle, and store the rice. Through selective breeding, wild rice plants evolved from branched and bushy plants to taller plants with a central stalk. This allowed farmers to grow more plants together and so increase the amount of rice they harvested.

> **People selected rice plants without anthocyanins for future crops. Although the rice tasted better, it was also more vulnerable to pests and disease.**

Although most scientists believe that the earliest domestication of rice occurred in China's Lower Yangtze River Valley, there is some evidence that rice was independently domesticated in other parts of Asia and India.

Golden Rice

Golden rice is a new variety of rice created by genetic engineering. Scientists used genetic engineering to add beta-carotene to rice. The beta-carotene gives golden rice a yellow-orange color. Beta-carotene is a plant pigment that the human body converts into vitamin A. Worldwide, vitamin A deficiency is a serious health problem that can lead to blindness and weaken the body's defenses to disease and infection. Golden rice tastes the same as regular rice but provides up to 30 to 50 percent of the vitamin A that humans require.

Scientists have traced a variety of long, dry grains to the Brahmaputra River Valley near the Himalayas. Other research suggests that another variety of rice emerged in the region near modern India and Bangladesh.

GROWING RICE

Rice plants require particular growing conditions. Young rice plants need massive amounts of water. Early farmers in China's Yangtze River Valley developed a way of growing rice in **paddy fields**. A paddy field is a flat field flooded with water. Rivers and rainfall flood many rice paddies in Asia during the monsoon season. Others must be irrigated to bring in the water that the rice needs.

Most paddies hold about 4 to 6 inches of water. Rice paddies are flooded for about 75 percent of the growing season before the water recedes.

In some parts of Asia, large areas of flat land for growing rice were not available. Some rice farmers found a solution by building step-like **terraces** into hills and mountains. Each terrace became a small, flat rice field. When it rained, the rain flowed down the steps. Each step channeled water to the next step. Soil nutrients were not lost in the rain but were carried to the plants on the next terrace. Terracing also prevented **erosion**, keeping the soil from being washed away in heavy rainfall or flooding.

THE SCIENCE OF SEEDS

RICE IN CHINA

Rice has been essential to Chinese civilizations and culture for thousands of years. The Chinese have many myths and legends about rice and its origins. In one myth, China suffered from severe floods from the waters of the Yellow River. To escape the floodwaters, the Chinese people fled to the hills. When the floodwaters receded, they returned to their homes and discovered that all the plants had been destroyed and very little food remained.

Then, a dog arrived, carrying yellow seeds on its tail. The Chinese people planted the yellow seeds, and they grew into rice plants. With enough rice to eat, the people thrived.

There are more than 40,000 different varieties of cultivated rice.

The Yangtze River in China

By 1100 BCE in the Western Zhou Dynasty (1100 BCE–771 BCE), rice had become a vital crop in China. Rice was an essential source of food. Rice was also used for trade and even as a **currency**. Many believed rice symbolized fertility and good luck. They used rice in religious ceremonies and festivals. Rice was even used to make wine. Many bronze storage vessels made during that time bore **inscriptions** about storing rice. These inscriptions show how essential rice was to the Chinese diet.

In China, rice was primarily grown in the south, where the land was most fertile. As the demand for rice grew in northern China, the Chinese began building a massive canal in 468 BCE. The Grand Canal linked the southern city of Hangzhou with Beijing in the north. It stretched 1,115 miles and linked several rivers across China. Rice and other materials traveled on the canal from the south to supply the north. Since then, the canal has been expanded several times.

Take a bird's eye view of rice terraces in the remote Cordillera mountain range in the Philippines. Why do certain foods hold both cultural importance and economic importance?

🔎 Nat Geo rice terraces

The reliance on agriculture and rice farming became a way of life for many Chinese people. Rice farmers plowed fields in the spring and weeded in the summer. They harvested in the fall and lived off stored food supplies during the winter. Large pieces of land could be successfully used for rice farming, and most Chinese worked the land in some way.

RICE IN CHINESE FESTIVALS

Rice played an important role in several traditional Chinese festivals and rituals. Many of these traditions are still followed today. For example, during the Spring Festival, also known as the Lunar New Year, the Chinese eat a sweet **nian gao** cake. The cake is made with glutinous rice flour, which is sticky.

zongzi: sticky rice dumplings traditionally eaten during the Chinese Dragon Boat Festival.

The cake symbolizes people's wishes for a better future. They eat the cake for good luck in the new year.

In another tradition, Chinese people make rice dumplings on the 15th night of the first lunar month. This day is the first day the full moon can be seen in the new year. Eating the dumplings is thought to bring good luck.

At the annual Dragon Boat Festival, sticky rice dumplings called **zongzi** are a highlight. This festival takes place on the fifth day of the fifth lunar month of the year. Zongzi are made from sticky rice and filled with sweet or savory fillings. Traditionally wrapped in bamboo or reed leaves, zongzi can be made in different shapes based on local customs.

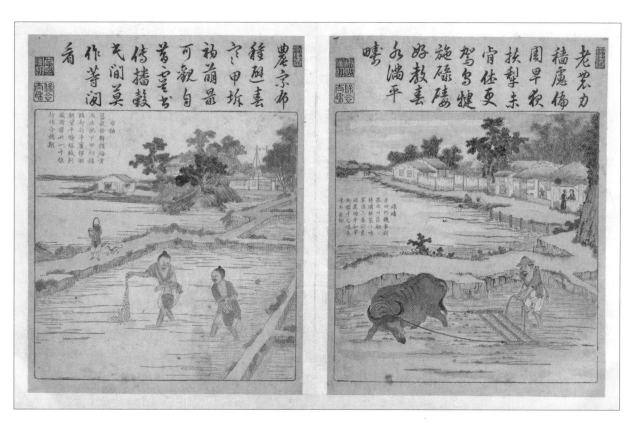

Scenes from a rice field, Kangxi, Emperor of China, Zhuan, Shu, and Chinese Rare Book Collection. Yu Zhi Geng Zhi Tu. 1723

Rice in Africa

African rice, called Oryza glaberrima, was domesticated in West Africa more than 3,000 years ago. Later, it spread from West Africa throughout the continent. African rice has a reddish color and a nutty flavor. Compared to Asian rice, African rice better tolerates changes in water depth, infertile soils, severe climate conditions, and drought. Some varieties of African rice mature more quickly and can be planted directly on the ground without using seedlings. Today, rice is grown in about 40 countries in Africa.

Listen to the African Plant Hunter talk about African rice. Why might this crop make a comeback?

🔍 African Plant Hunter rice

According to legend, people eat zongzi during the festival to remember Qu Yuan, an official with the state of Chu during the Warring States Period (475–221 BCE). After the capital of Chu was defeated by the state of Qin, Qu Yuan jumped into the Miluo River and died. People threw sticky rice dumplings into the river to prevent the fish from eating his body. Since then, rice dumplings have been an important part of the Dragon Boat Festival.

The Great Wall of China was built with rice. During the fifteenth and sixteenth centuries, workers mixed a porridge made of rice and calcium carbonate that was used as a mortar to hold the wall's stones together.

RICE SPREADS AROUND THE WORLD

Rice farming spread from China through southeastern Asia. Archaeological evidence suggests that rice farmers from China migrated to other parts of Asia, bringing rice seeds and farming practices. They taught hunter-gatherer people in new regions how to cultivate rice.

WORDS TO KNOW

humid: having a high level of moisture in the air.

plantation: a large farm where one crop is often grown.

habitat: the natural area where a plant or animal lives.

From southeastern Asia, rice spread through Sri Lanka and India and then to Greece, Sicily, and the surrounding Mediterranean region. From there, rice spread gradually through southern Europe and northern Africa.

Brown rice is also a good source of fiber.

European explorers and settlers brought rice to the New World, introducing it in several locations across Central and South America. Rice appeared in the North American colonies during the late 1600s. The South Carolina and Georgia colonies provided a warm, **humid** environment for growing rice, so some wealthy farmers established rice **plantations** there. Enslaved people from Africa's west coast brought their knowledge of how to cultivate rice. They labored on the many rice plantations in the region and produced valuable commercial crops.

After the American Civil War, Carolina rice plantations struggled without the labor of enslaved people. Eventually, rice farming declined in the Carolinas. Today, American rice farmers grow about 20 billion pounds annually in Arkansas, California, Louisiana, Mississippi, Missouri, and Texas. That's only about 2 percent of the world's rice production! But almost 45 percent of that is exported to other countries every year.

Wildlife Habitat

In the United States, millions of acres of rice fields create an essential wetland **habitat** for many species. The fields are home to many waterfowl, including ducks, geese, herons, egrets, pelicans, and more. For the threatened black-necked stilt, the rice fields provide an important habitat. This shorebird walks through the wetlands in search of insects, shrimp, crayfish, snails, tadpoles, and other small animals that live on or near the water surface.

THE GREEN REVOLUTION AND RICE

Asia, home to 50 percent of the world's population, faced a food crisis during the mid-1900s. Asian people depended on rice, which made up 80 percent of the calories in their diet. Yet the region's population was growing much faster than its rice production. Scientists predicted food shortages within a few years.

To find a solution, two American charities, the Ford and Rockefeller Foundations, joined together in 1960. They established the International Rice Research Institute (IRRI) in the Philippines. The IRRI's main goal was to create a rice hybrid plant that would produce higher yields, just as Borlaug had done with wheat. They hoped high-yield rice would help the world avoid a food crisis.

Always store cooked rice in the refrigerator. When cooked rice is left at room temperature, spores in the rice that survived cooking can grow bacteria, which can eventually cause food poisoning.

IR8: A HYBRID RICE

A team of scientists got to work. They methodically cross-bred 10,000 different varieties of rice. Eventually, they crossed a tall, high-yield rice strain from Indonesia with a sturdy dwarf plant from China. The results were stunning.

According to some studies, the resulting hybrid rice, named IR8, could produce 10 times the amount of rice as traditional varieties. Such a significant increase in yield had never been seen before. IR8 was nicknamed the "miracle rice." The new hybrid variety was short, which allowed the plant to use the sun's energy to produce more grains instead of using it to grow taller. The shorter plant was also more resistant to weather and disease.

Manoomin is a traditional wild rice for many Indigenous peoples in Minnesota and the surrounding region. Watch this video to see how people have harvested this rice for generations. Why is it important to practice traditional agriculture even as technology becomes more advanced?

🔎 Minnesota Historical wild rice harvesting

The new hybrid IR8 was released in 1966. IR8 performed so much better than traditional rice plants that farmers throughout Asia quickly began using it. Rice output skyrocketed.

Famine was avoided. Farmers benefited from increased productivity, while consumers enjoyed lower rice prices.

However, there were some drawbacks to IR8. As more farmers began growing IR8, it quickly became the only variety of rice grown in some parts of Asia. Relying on a single variety reduced biodiversity and increased the risk of disaster if a pest, disease, or extreme weather destroyed the crop. IR8 also led to a significant increase in the use of chemical fertilizers, which created harmful environmental side effects.

The IR8 variety did not taste as good as traditional rice varieties. It was chalky and hardened after cooking. The IRRI scientists spent the next 20 years improving IR8.

Today, the IRRI continues to develop new and improved rice varieties. The IRRI has a cold storage unit that holds approximately 80,000 rice samples. It can use these samples to create new rice varieties. Much of the IRRI's work is focused on developing rice that can adapt to Earth's changing climate. For example, scientists are developing strains of rice that can resist drought, flooding, salt, and extreme temperatures.

MANY VARIETIES OF RICE

Today, rice is one of the world's largest crops, along with maize and wheat. There are more than 40,000 varieties of cultivated rice worldwide. Most rice can be grouped into two main categories: Indica and Japonica. Indica rice varieties are typically long grain, while Japonica rice varieties are short grain. People depend on rice because it is a nutritious food source with energy-rich carbohydrates, vitamins, and minerals.

TEXT TO **WORLD**

Does your family eat certain foods on special days, such as holidays? What are the stories behind those foods?

THE SCIENCE OF SEEDS

White rice is one of the common varieties of rice in the world. It is also the most processed, with the grain's husk, bran, and germ removed. Removing these parts of the rice grain also removes much of its essential nutrients. White rice contains less protein and nutrients than other rice varieties. It is also less filling, because much of its fiber has been removed.

Only the husk is removed from brown rice. Brown rice retains more **antioxidants**, nutrients, fiber, and protein than white rice. Similarly, red and black rice contain more fiber and nutrients than white rice. Red rice is rich in iron and **flavonoids** that have health benefits such as reducing inflammation and improving heart health. Black rice is rich in protein, fiber, and vitamin E, which reduce the risk of certain cancers and other diseases.

Some common varieties of rice include arborio, basmati, and jasmine. Arborio rice has a medium grain and a high starch content and is slightly chewy and sticky, which makes it a good choice for risotto and soups. Basmati rice is a long grain rice with a nutty flavor. It is commonly used in Indian and Asian cooking. Jasmine rice, another long grain rice, has a floral, nutty flavor and a moist, soft texture when cooked. It is often used in Asian cooking, including stir-fries and curries.

MODERN RICE FARMS

Read this article to learn more about different types of rice that you might see in the grocery store. How many have you tried?

🔎 Consumer Reports rice type

Today, farmers use modern technology to cultivate rice. In the United States, computerized, laser-guided equipment levels the land to ensure rice fields are flat. Farmers plant seeds in the early spring using grain drills pulled by a tractor. Some farms cast seeds over dry or flooded fields by airplane.

Wild Rice

Today, many people eat the long, black grains of wild rice. Yet this wild rice is not rice at all. It is an aquatic grass! Wild rice grows in waterways throughout the United States, especially near the Great Lakes. In some places, its stalks can grow up to 12 feet (3.6 meters) tall. Compared to traditional white and brown rice, wild rice has long, black grains that have thicker and more rigid hulls. The flavor of wild rice is nutty and earthy. It makes a delicious addition to many meals.

Depending on the region, rice fields are flooded between March and May. This provides a wetland habitat for hundreds of species of birds, amphibians, and mammals.

By fall, the rice is ready for harvest. Farmers drain the fields and use combines to harvest the crop. During harvest, farmers remove the heads of the rice plants, leaving only the stems, which they later cut and bale as straw. The rough rice is put through a dryer, where moisture is removed from each grain. The dried rough rice goes to a mill for processing. A rice huller removes the outer husk, called a **chaff**, from the rough rice, creating brown rice. The brown outer layers, called bran, are removed to create white rice.

Advances in **biotechnology** and genetic engineering have made it possible for scientists to transfer genes from one rice plant directly into the cells of another plant. Instead of cross-breeding plants by hand, scientists can now make specific changes to the genes of plants in a lab. However, not everyone agrees that changing the genes of rice plants is a good idea. Some people worry that changing the genes of foods we eat might have harmful long-term effects for human health and the environment.

In the next chapter, we'll look at another popular food that has changed through time: potatoes!

ESSENTIAL QUESTION

Why is it important for new varieties of rice to be both tasty and healthy?

SELECTIVE BREEDING

Humans have practiced selective breeding for thousands of years. Selective breeding allowed people to breed animals and plants so they had certain characteristics. They chose cows that produced more milk and dogs that were smaller in size.

Many of today's dog breeds exist because people wanted dogs with specific characteristics to perform tasks such as retrieving, protection, assistance, hunting, companionship, and more. In this activity, you will use selective breeding to create a new breed of dog.

> **Brainstorm a task that the new dog breed will perform.** Think about the characteristics that would help the dog be most successful in its role. Choose at least three characteristics. What existing dog breeds have some of those characteristics?

> **What two existing dog breeds would be the best parents for a puppy with the characteristics you want?** Choose the mother and father.

> **In a litter of three puppies, each puppy will inherit traits from either the mother or father.** For this activity, you can flip a coin to determine if the puppy inherits the mother's trait (heads) or the father's (tails). Flip the coin for each trait, for each puppy. Record the results.

> **Consider what each puppy is like.** How are they similar? How are they different? Which puppy do you think will be best able to perform the desired task?

> **To selectively breed another generation of your dog, pick the puppy you want as one of the parents.** Why choose that puppy?

The dachshund is one example of a dog breed that was created to perform a specific job. Find out more about why the dachshund was created in this American Kennel Club article.

🔎 AKC dachshund

Consider This!

Selective breeding can produce offspring with desired characteristics. But it also can have some drawbacks. What are the disadvantages of selective breeding?

BAKE
NIAN GAO

Nian gao is a simple, sweet cake that is often eaten during the Chinese New Year to bring good luck. Nian gao is made from glutinous rice flour and sugar. In one Chinese legend, nian gao was made as an offering to the Kitchen God, who was believed to live in every house. At the end of the year, the Kitchen God made a yearly report to the Jade Emperor. When people served nian gao to the Kitchen God, the sweet cake stuck his mouth together, making him unable to give a bad report on their house. In this activity, you will make a simple version of nian gao.

Ask an adult to help you with the stove and mixer!

> **Traditional nian gao is steamed, but this version of the cake is baked.** Preheat an oven to 350 degrees Fahrenheit. Grease two 8-inch round baking pans. Do not use non-stick pans.

> **Beat the eggs and brown sugar together in a mixing bowl.** Slowly mix in the rice flour. Add the coconut milk and water and mix until the batter is smooth.

> **Pour the batter into the baking pans.**

> **Bake the cakes in the oven for 45 minutes.** Insert a toothpick into the center to test that the cakes are fully baked.

> **Broil in the oven for 2 to 3 minutes.** The cakes should turn a light brown color.

> **Carefully remove from the oven and transfer to a cooling rack.** Let cool for at least an hour before cutting and serving.

Consider This!

Does your family have a special cake or food served for a holiday you celebrate? What is it made from? What does the food represent?

WHAT TYPE OF RICE?

Today, there are more than 40,000 varieties of rice. Can you spot the difference?

Ask an adult for help cooking the rice.

> **Pour some grains of rice on a paper plate.** Use the magnifying glass to study the rice. Record your observations of the size, shape, color, and texture of the rice. Repeat for each type of rice.

* What characteristics does each type have that make it different from the others?

* What is each type of rice primarily used for?

> **Cook a small amount of each kind of rice, following the directions on the packaging.** How does each kind of rice taste different? Are some kinds of rice stickier than others?

> **Using your notes, create a chart or table that highlights the types of rice and their characteristics.**

Type	Size	Shape	Color	Texture

Consider This!

Show your chart to your family or friends and see if they can use your descriptions and observations of the rice grains to identify the different types of rice.

Chapter 5

POTATOES

What would meatloaf be without a side of mashed potatoes? Imagine eating a hamburger without hot, crispy French fries. And snack time without potato chips?! Many of our favorite foods would not be possible without the potato. The simple potato has sprung from the ground to become one of the world's most important food crops.

The potato is one of the world's four main staple crops, along with maize, wheat, and rice. People love potatoes so much for many reasons. First, potatoes are simple to plant and harvest. Farmers do not need a lot of complicated equipment—they can use a simple spade to plant, weed, and dig up potatoes. You can even grow potatoes in your backyard! Potato plants grow well in places where other staple crops do not, such as at high elevations and in dry climates. And the potato has a short growing season of about 75 days.

ESSENTIAL QUESTION

Why do we need to keep seeking new solutions to blight, pests, and other threats to crops?

In addition to being easy to grow, potato plants produce a lot of food. A single potato plant produces an average of 4.4 pounds of potatoes each season. And some potato plants produce a lot more. One English farmer holds a Guinness World Record for producing more than 370 pounds of potatoes from a single plant.

As a staple food, potatoes are nutritious. They are a good source of vitamins and minerals, including vitamins C and B6, iron, potassium, and zinc. The potato skin can be eaten and provides dietary fiber. Potatoes are low in sodium and have no fat or cholesterol, which makes them a healthy part of a balanced diet. Be aware, however, that some ways of preparing potatoes can make them less healthy for you.

Whether boiled, baked, or fried, potatoes have become part of dishes worldwide. So, where did this simple spud come from, and how did it become one of the most important foods in the world?

In 1995, potatoes became the first vegetable grown in space. Scientists are learning how to grow many different kinds of crops in space to make longer space flight possible and more comfortable!

Vegetative Propagation

Vegetative propagation is a method of plant reproduction. It occurs when new plants grow from a parent plant's roots, stem, or leaves. Vegetative propagation is a form of **asexual** reproduction because it does not involve any reproductive organ. For potatoes, new potato plants grow from pieces of swollen roots called tubers. These tubers are what we know as potatoes. The new plants are genetically identical to the parent plants and can be cultivated faster than growing a new plant from seeds. However, because the new plants are genetically identical, they are at increased risk of a single disease wiping them all out.

A SOUTH AMERICAN BEGINNING

The story of the potato began about 12,000 years ago in South America. Indigenous people living in South America hunted and gathered food to survive. Among the edible wild plants that they gathered were more than 200 different species of potatoes.

The word "potato" comes from the Spanish word *patata*. The word "patata" comes from the Taino word *batata*.

South America's Andes Mountains are one of the world's longest and highest mountain ranges. The region near the mountains has very little flat land. Scientists believe that Andean farmers were able to domesticate the potato between 7,000 and 10,000 years ago. Potato domestication most likely occurred in the Lake Titicaca basin, an area near the border of modern-day Bolivia and Peru. Wild potato plants grew around the lake.

The Andean farmers probably took these wild potato plants and learned to grow them through trial and error. They discovered that new potato plants could be grown simply by planting a piece of the potato, a process called vegetative propagation.

WORDS TO KNOW

llama: a long-necked, South American pack animal.

alpaca: a long-haired, South American mammal.

togosh: a traditional Inca food prepared from fermented potato pulp.

chuño: a freeze-dried potato product developed by the Inca people.

Wild potato plants produced potatoes in various shapes, sizes, colors, and tastes. When the Andean farmers found a potato they liked, they planted a piece of it. This method produced new plants that were identical to the original plant. In this way, the early potato farmers grew many varieties of potatoes. Since then, thousands of domesticated potato varieties have been developed. As a result, potatoes are one of the world's most varied domesticated crops.

The Andes have little flat land for farming, so people built terraces on the steep mountain sides. Using wooden spades and sticks, they planted the potatoes in the hard, rocky soil. Potatoes grew in valleys and on the mountain terraces.

Manure from the local **llamas** and **alpacas** fertilized the potato plants. With hand axes, early farmers dug up and harvested the ripe potatoes. The Andean farmers valued the potato for its ability to grow at high altitudes and to be stored for long periods. The success of potato crops and maize allowed civilizations to grow and thrive around the Lake Titicaca area between 500 and 800 CE.

> **How do commercial farms plant their potato crops?** Watch this video to see how they do it. Why do you think potatoes are such a popular food?
>
> ○ Eat Happy Project potatoes

INCA EMPIRE

Around 1200 CE, the Inca people founded a small kingdom in the Andes Mountains. The Inca gradually conquered nearby people and built an empire that, at its peak, reached about 2,000 miles from central Chile to southern Colombia. The Inca empire had a population of between 9 and 15 million people. At the time, they were the largest and fastest-growing civilization in the Americas. The potato played a large part in sustaining the Inca people.

Chuño, an Inca freeze-dried potato dish

The potato became a staple of the Inca diet. It fed people across the empire and gave strength to the Inca armies. The Inca boiled, mashed, and roasted potatoes. They fermented potatoes in water to make a sticky food called **togosh**.

The Inca ground dried potato into flour and baked it into bread. They added potatoes to soups and stews. They also ate potatoes with meat and other vegetables.

The Inca developed a way to preserve the potato crop after harvest to prevent mold and decay. After harvesting, the farmers covered the potatoes and left them outside overnight in freezing temperatures. The next day, the potatoes were set out in the sun. The people stomped on the frozen potatoes to squeeze out liquid. This process was repeated several times over the following days. The result was a freeze-dried potato product called **chuño**, which they stored in sealed, underground warehouses. Chuño could be stored for 10 to 15 years, providing a stockpile of food to prevent future famines.

Potatoes had other uses in the Inca civilization. The Inca used potatoes to treat injuries. They attached raw potato slices to broken bones. If a person had a stomachache, they ate potato. If they had a sore throat, they'd tie a piece of potato around their neck. The Inca also believed that potatoes made childbirth easier.

Potatoes also had a role in the Incan religious beliefs and practices. The Inca were polytheistic, which meant they worshipped many gods. In the Inca religion, gods controlled the elements of nature, including the sun, moon, and rain. In Inca myth, Axomamma was the goddess of potatoes. The people prayed to Axomamma, and many villages had an odd-shaped potato they worshipped so that Axomamma would bless them with a good harvest.

There is a potato museum in Idaho. And yes, it has a cafe.

THE POTATO MIGRATES

During the 1530s, Spanish explorers arrived in the Andes. They likely first encountered the potato in an Inca village as they searched for gold in the New World. The Spanish explorers saw the Inca eating potatoes and gradually began using potatoes to feed sailors on their ships. They took potatoes and other New World crops, such as tomatoes and maize, across the Atlantic Ocean in what is known as the Great Columbian Exchange. This involved the movement of people, animals, plants, and diseases between Europe and the Americas. Some Spanish farmers began to grow potatoes, mainly to feed their livestock.

The potato slowly spread from Spain to Italy and other European countries during the late 1500s. However, people did not immediately embrace the new food in many places. They looked at the funny-shaped tubers with suspicion. They believed potatoes were unfit for humans and should be fed only to animals.

Eventually, Europeans recognized the value of the potato. Potatoes provided nutrition and satisfied hunger. They did not spoil as quickly as other crops and were inexpensive to cultivate. Potatoes grew well in northern European climates and adapted to different soil conditions. They were easy for farmers to cultivate with only a few hand tools. Within a few months, the potato plants matured and produced a plentiful and nutritious food crop.

Who invented French fries? There's an argument about that! Watch this video about the history of French fries. Why is language so important in food history?

🔎 history French fries now and then

For the people caught in Europe's wars, potatoes had another advantage. They were hard to see. Fields of grain crops such as wheat were difficult to hide from hungry soldiers. But potatoes grew underground. The ability to dig up potatoes a few at a time protected food supplies during wartime. Enemy soldiers often emptied grain stores and destroyed field crops, but they rarely took the time to dig up potato crops.

By the 1800s, the potato had become a valued food reserve in Europe.

THE SCIENCE OF SEEDS

Arriving in Ireland in the late 1500s, potatoes thrived in the Irish soil and climate. The Irish began planting potatoes as a field crop during the 1600s. Irish farmers selected favorable plants to create a potato variety that could produce tubers earlier in the summer. By the 1700s, the Irish embraced potatoes as a staple food. They saw the potato as a way to protect their growing population from famine.

Potatoes arrived in the American colonies during the 1620s. The British governor of the Bahamas sent a box of potatoes as a gift to the governor of Virginia. But the tuber was not widely accepted until President Thomas Jefferson reportedly served potatoes to his guests at the White House. During the mid-1700s, immigrants from Scotland, Ireland, and other European countries brought potatoes to the United States and planted them as field crops. By the mid-1800s, potatoes had become an important field crop in the United States and Canada.

From Europe, potatoes also spread to Africa, Asia, and the South Pacific. During the 1900s, the potato became the world's most cultivated and eaten vegetable.

> Take a peek under the soil to see how a potato grows in time lapse! Why do you need to leave space between seed potatoes?
>
> 🔎 Beneath the soil Potato tuber time lapse

POPULATIONS GROW

With potato crops, Europe's farmers could produce much more food. Potatoes also provided insurance in case wheat or other grain crops failed. Potatoes provided the vitamins and minerals the human body needed for better health. With a plentiful, nutritious food supply, birth rates rose and **mortality** rates dropped. In England, potatoes were a cheap source of calories and nutrients for urban workers in Industrial Revolution factories during the 1800s. After people adopted the potato, populations in Europe and the United States boomed.

Ireland is one example of a country where the potato significantly impacted the population. The number of people in Ireland doubled to 8 million between 1780 and 1841.

During this time, the potato became a staple food. There was no significant change in Irish industry or farming techniques except for widespread potato farming. At the time, many Irish people rented tiny plots of land from landowners and planted potatoes. Because the potato produced so much food, even the poorest Irish farmers could produce enough nutritious food with one milking cow and an acre of potatoes to feed their families. Potato crops were easy to plant, harvest, and cook, and they appeared on every Irish table.

In France, Marie Antoinette wore potato blossoms in her hair, making the potato a fashionable spud.

POTATO FAMINE

In 1842, farmers near Philadelphia, Pennsylvania, noticed something was wrong with their potato plants. The leaves curled, and the plant bodies wilted. The farmers dug up the potatoes and found brown streaks throughout them. Later, the potatoes blackened and became slimy. The farmers had no idea what disease or pest was attacking their potatoes. But they quickly discovered that once part of the crop had **blight**, the entire crop could be destroyed in mere days.

The potato blight, called "potato rot," spread quickly. Potato crops in Pennsylvania, New York, and Massachusetts died. For the Americans, the loss of potato crops was troubling but not an emergency.

People ate potatoes regularly, but few people relied on potatoes alone. Most farmers replaced their potatoes with other crops.

In 1844, the potato blight appeared in Belgium. With no known cure or way to prevent it, blight spread quickly through the Netherlands, Scandinavia, France, Germany, Prussia, and Russia. In some countries, farmers planted grain crops to replace the potatoes. The impact was much more severe for those who relied solely on potatoes. Hundreds of thousands of people in mainland Europe died from starvation.

Colorado Potato Beetle

credit: U.S. Department of Agriculture (CC BY 2.0)

During the 1860s, American farmers encountered a new pest—the Colorado potato beetle. Because farmers planted just a few varieties of potato, pests such as the beetle and blight could easily wipe out entire fields. Farmers tried everything they could think of to get rid of the beetles. Eventually, one man threw some leftover green paint on his beetle-infested potato plants. Amazingly, the paint killed the beetles. The paint's green color came from a pigment called Paris green, made from **arsenic** and copper. Even though arsenic is **toxic**, farmers began spraying a solution of the paint on their plants. During the late 1800s and 1900s, scientists tried using Paris green and other chemicals to protect potatoes and other crops from pests and disease. They had to keep coming up with new pesticides because the potato beetle was very good at developing a resistance to any chemical thrown at it! More pesticides and insecticides were developed to protect potato plants and other crops from damage caused by pests and diseases. The modern pesticide industry was born.

IRISH POTATO FAMINE

In 1845, the potato blight spread to England, Scotland, and Ireland. In England and Scotland, the loss of potatoes was felt, but the countries were able to avoid significant famine. In Ireland, however, a major disaster loomed.

The potato was more than an important food in Ireland. In many homes and villages, it was the only food. Many Irish people, particularly in rural areas, survived on milk and potatoes, which provided the essential nutrients they needed.

In the Andes Mountains, the "Potato King" grows more than 400 native varieties of potato. Watch his story here. What does it mean to have a deep connection on the land where you live?

⌕ Farmer Growing 400 Different Kinds of Potatoes

At the same time, the Irish population had skyrocketed during the first half of the century. Many relied on potato crops to earn money to pay rent on farms and homes. If the potato crops were poor, people had no other crop to harvest in its place. Their dependence on a single food crop set the stage for disaster.

Ireland continued to export wheat and other crops even as Irish families starved to death.

Once the potato blight arrived in Ireland, it spread quickly. Within weeks, some people began to warn of an impending famine. In 1845, the blight cut the Irish potato harvest by about 30 percent. And it would only get worse. By 1846, the blight had spread throughout Ireland, and nearly 90 percent of the Irish potato crop was destroyed. Famine and disease followed closely behind the blight.

The Irish potato famine ended in 1851. By then, more than 1 million Irish people had died from starvation and disease. Millions more left Ireland, with many coming to North America. Ireland's population dropped from about 8 million in 1841 to 4 million by 1900.

THE SCIENCE OF SEEDS

WORDS TO KNOW

fungus: a simple organism that is neither plant nor animal and includes mushrooms, yeasts, and molds.

fungicide: a chemical that destroys fungus.

versatile: able to be used in lots of ways.

dehydrate: to take the water out of something.

During the 1800s, no one knew what caused the potato blight. Some believed wet weather triggered it. Others blamed poor soil. Some religious people believed God had sent the blight to punish Catholics living in Ireland. Eventually, scientists discovered the guilty party: a **fungus**. Today, DNA research has led many scientists to suspect the fungus most likely originated in South America and spread to the United States. Then, the fungus hitched a ride on potatoes carried in ships across the Atlantic Ocean to Europe.

Today, potato blight still exists. Every year, millions of tons of potatoes are lost to blight. Farmers are better, however, at rotating crops and carefully using **fungicides** to help control it.

A VERSATILE SPUD

The potato belongs to the nightshade family, which includes tomatoes and peppers.

For hundreds of years, the potato has fed people worldwide. One of the reasons why people enjoy the popular spud is because it is so **versatile**. You can boil, fry, bake, and roast potatoes. You can serve them whole, sliced, or diced. Potatoes can be part of any meal, from hash browns at breakfast to potato salad at lunch and French fries at dinner.

Potato starch and potato flour, made from **dehydrated** potatoes, are used in the food industry to thicken soups and gravies. Potato starch is also a binding agent in cakes, doughs, biscuits, and ice cream. People even use potatoes to make alcoholic beverages such as vodka—when crushed potatoes are heated, the starch in them is converted to fermentable sugars.

Today, the simple potato is used in a variety of non-food products. Potato starch is widely used as an adhesive, binder, texture agent, and filler in medicines, chemicals, animal feed, wood, and paper. Potato starch is also a biodegradable substitute for some plastics used in disposable plates, dishes, and knives. And on farms worldwide, potatoes are used as animal feed.

Potatoes can even be used to make an industrial chemical called ethanol. Ethanol can be used as a renewable biofuel. Currently, U.S. gasoline is mixed with some ethanol, reducing air pollution. Potato peels and other wastes from potato processing contain a lot of starch. To produce ethanol, the starch is liquefied and fermented.

Today, most potatoes are grown and consumed in developing countries. In 2021, 376 million metric tons of potatoes were produced globally. China and India were the two largest potato-producing countries, with 94 million metric tons and 54 million metric tons, respectively. Across Africa and Asia, the potato has become a staple crop in several countries, including Ethiopia, Uganda, India, Bangladesh, Indonesia, Vietnam, and China.

TEXT TO **WORLD**

What is your favorite form of cooked potato? Where was that type of cooking invented?

POTATO RESEARCH TODAY

During the late 1800s, scientists launched several potato research centers in Europe and North America. At these centers, plant scientists studied potato breeding. They produced several new productive varieties of the potato plant. Through the years, they have worked to produce better potato varieties that could help developing countries improve food security.

Some potato research has centered on genetic engineering. Scientists have developed a genetically modified potato with reduced browning and bruising. Browning and bruising can occur when a potato is stored, transported, or cut in the kitchen. Although browning and bruising affect only a potato's look, they can lead to food waste because people throw away perfectly good potatoes.

Don't eat green potatoes! These potatoes have been exposed to too much sunlight and might make you sick.

GMO potatoes also produce less of a chemical called asparagine. If you cook potatoes at high heat, such as when cooking cut potatoes in a high-heat fryer to make French fries, the asparagine is converted to a chemical called acrylamide, which can potentially cause cancer. Because GMO potatoes have less asparagine, they can be fried at high heat without people worrying about producing cancer-causing chemicals.

We've learned a lot about four staple crops—maize, wheat, rice, and potatoes. These are the foods that have most helped shape the world into what we know. What about other crops? Are there any that have gone extinct, just like dinosaurs and some mammals? Are there any in danger of going extinct? Let's take a look.

ESSENTIAL QUESTION

Why do we need to keep seeking new solutions to blight, pests, and other threats to crops?

GROW A
POTATO IN WATER

One reason why potatoes have become so popular worldwide is that they are easy to grow. All you need to grow a new potato plant is a piece of an old potato, water, and soil. This process is called vegetative propagation. In this activity, we will see how a new plant starts using water.

> Push the toothpicks into the middle of the potato. The toothpicks should stick out all around the potato.

> Place the potato in the cup. The toothpicks should rest on the top of the cup while the potato hangs down into the cup.

> Pour water into the cup. It should cover the bottom half of the potato.

> Place the cup with the potato and water in a dark, cool place. Leave it there for a week or two until sprouts begin to grow.

Try This!

Transplant the sprouting potato into soil. You can use a container or a backyard garden. How many new potatoes can you grow?

> After the potato has sprouted, move the cup near a sunny window. Check on the potato daily and add water to the cup as needed. You will see shoots and roots growing.

> Record your observations and compare your results with classmates.

Potato Flowers

Potato plants can produce flowers—but that process depends on the temperature and amount of nutrients the plant gets. Those flowers can even produce berries, and inside those berries you'll find seeds. Plant the seeds and you might even get potatoes. But unlike those planted from tuber, these potatoes will be genetically different from the parent plant. And they'll take much longer to grow.

POTATOES
IN ART

Throughout history, potatoes have been featured in art. Artists such as Jean-Francois Millet, Vincent Van Gogh, and Jacqueline De Jong incorporated potatoes in several of their paintings. Why do you think the potato was an important subject for these artists?

❯ **Choose an artist who featured potatoes in their art.** You can pick one of the artists mentioned above or another one of your choosing. Research the artist and their work. As you research, think about the following questions.

✱ What is the artist's background?

✱ What materials does the artist use?

✱ What is the artist's style or genre?

✱ What inspires the artist? Who or what influenced them?

✱ How did the artist use potatoes in their artwork?

✱ What meaning do you think the artist intended for this artwork?

❯ **Create a slide presentation for your class to share what you have learned.**

Try This!

Create your own piece of art featuring a potato. How will you portray the potato? What meaning do you wish to convey with your art?

Chapter 6

ENDANGERED SEEDS

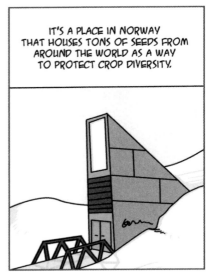

Norway's island of Spitsbergen sits in the middle of the cold Arctic Ocean. The remote island is part of an **archipelago** between mainland Norway and the North Pole. It experiences near-total daylight in the summer and darkness in the winter.

ESSENTIAL QUESTION

Why is it important to maintain diversity in our seed supply?

On the island, a gray building sticks out from a snow-covered mountainside. A small metal bridge leads to its entrance. Above the entrance, a green light glows. On the building's side, large letters reveal that it is the "Svalbard Global Seed Vault."

WORDS TO KNOW

archipelago: a group of islands.

99

THE SCIENCE OF SEEDS

The vault is closed to the public and only a few people are allowed inside its metal doors. These restrictions keep the vault's precious contents safe. The seed vault holds more than 1.2 million seed samples from almost every nation on Earth. Called by some the "doomsday seed vault," Svalbard protects crop biodiversity. By doing so, the seed vault is the world's last line of defense against **catastrophic** crop failures on Earth.

WHAT IS CROP DIVERSITY?

Take a virtual tour of the Svalbard Global Seed Vault at this website. Why are seed banks important? What does it say about humans that we build a place for seeds to survive?

virtual global seed vault tour

PS

The Irish potato famine showed how reliance on a single crop for food could lead to catastrophe. To protect the world's food supply, crop diversity is essential. At its highest level, crop diversity means planting different crops on individual farms, as well as planting different crops on the national and global levels. Crop diversity also means planting different varieties of the same crop, such as many types of tomatoes.

On individual farms, crop diversity has many benefits. A farm with many different crops and several varieties within each crop will have improved soil health and quality. The farm as a whole will have a more resilient and healthier **ecosystem**. When bad weather, pests, or diseases affect one crop or one variety within a crop, the remaining crops are still productive. By growing more than one crop, individual farms are better protected when a specific crop fails.

On the national and global levels, crop diversity is essential for the staple crops that feed the world. Genetic diversity decreases when farms worldwide depend on just one or two crop varieties for food.

Crops with less genetic diversity have a higher risk of being affected by pests, disease, or other events that could cause crop failure. These less diverse crops make the world's food supply more vulnerable to catastrophe.

DECLINING DIVERSITY

Scientists have been warning about the decline in crop diversity for a century. Through the years, people all around the world have increasingly relied on a dwindling number of plants and animals for food. According to the Food and Agriculture Organization of the United Nations (FAO), 75 percent of the world's food comes from just 12 plant species and five animal species.

Seeds can stay dormant, or inactive, for many years. When conditions are good, they will germinate and begin to grow.

Svalbard Global Seed Vault in February 2020

credit: Cierra Martin for Crop Trust (CC BY SA 2.0)

THE SCIENCE OF SEEDS

Only three plant species—rice, maize, and wheat—make up nearly 60 percent of the plant-based calories humans consume.

And the genetic diversity of crops has also dipped. Since the 1900s, many farmers have stopped planting multiple varieties of crops. Instead, they have planted the same genetically identical, hybrid, high-yield varieties. As a result, about 75 percent of plant genetic diversity has been lost since 1900. For example, the number of rice varieties grown in Thailand has dropped from 16,000 to only 37.

Why do farmers grow the same type of crop year after year? As a society, we place value on knowing that the food we buy at the store is going to be the same as the food we bought last week. Farmers appreciate how much easier it is to grow what they know. But there's a price.

Polyculture Farming

Polyculture farming, or polycropping, is the practice of planting two or more crops on the same land at the same time. For example, a farmer might plant wheat and beans on the same field. The two crops can grow together and are easily separated after harvest. Polycropping is the opposite of **monocropping**. Planting different crops together attempts to recreate the biodiversity found naturally in ecosystems. Other benefits include nutrient sharing, pest control, and improved soil health. Remember the Native American practice of planting the Three Sisters? That's polyculture!

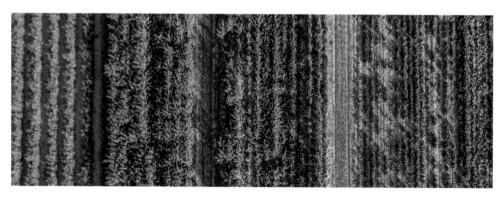

The significant decline in crop diversity concerns many people. As crop diversity declines, food systems become more vulnerable. More people depend on a few key crops, which leaves them more exposed to harvest failures. A failure of one of these key staple crops could trigger a devastating ripple effect throughout the global food system.

As Earth's climate changes, threats to the world's food supply are increasing. At the same time, the food system is less able to handle it. Weather patterns are changing, and extreme weather events are becoming more common. Pests and diseases are appearing in new areas. Growing conditions are becoming more unpredictable. Without crop and genetic diversity, it will be more difficult for key staple crops to adapt and thrive in Earth's changing environment.

Watch this video about the importance of saving seeds. Why is this a critical issue?

⌕ One Million Seed Savers PSA

MONOCROPPING: A THREAT TO CROP DIVERSITY

The practice of monocropping is one factor driving a decline in crop diversity. Monocropping means that farmers grow a single crop on the same land, season after season. The practice was intended to increase the food supply and reduce hunger worldwide. Farmers began monocropping to take advantage of new technologies and farming machinery designed to handle a specific crop. For example, the equipment needed to harvest wheat differs from what is needed to harvest soybeans. Each crop also needed specific combinations of pesticides and fertilizers. Planting a single crop that could use the same machinery and chemicals was more efficient.

For farmers, monocropping had benefits at first. They could plant one crop that produced more food and increased profits. And focusing on a single crop saved farmers time and money. A single machine designed for maize, wheat, or another crop could do the work of hundreds of human farm workers.

THE SCIENCE OF SEEDS

However, through time, monocropping has increased the risk of crop failure. Not all plants produce a good harvest every year. Pests, disease, and weather can strike without warning. On a farm with diverse crops, a threat to one crop may not affect another. A disease that affects wheat may not impact potatoes. But with a single crop, the entire field is vulnerable, especially when each plant is genetically the same as the one next to it. All it takes is one quickly spreading pest or a sudden hailstorm to destroy an entire field of crops. That is why nature builds diversity into Earth's living plants and animals.

Since 1900, nearly three species of seed-bearing plants have gone extinct each year.

PROTECTING CROP DIVERSITY

Think about what life would be like without maize, wheat, rice, or potatoes. It is almost impossible to imagine! That is why protecting crop diversity and the health of the world's staple crops is a global concern. It affects every person on the planet.

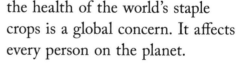

How are crops being genetically modified today? Watch this short video to find out. What might these modifications mean for the consumer?

U.S. Food and Drug Administration kinds of genetic modifications

The good news is that although crop diversity has declined, there are ways to protect and rebuild it. On farms, some solutions include planting different varieties of the same crop and planting different crops on the same land. Some plants can attract pests and keep them from harming food crops. Planting different plants also provides habitats for natural enemies of pests. Farmers can increase plant diversity by using trees, crops, and livestock on the same farm.

Rotating crops or planting different crops on the same land can improve soil health.

With improved soil, farmers need fewer chemical fertilizers. Plant diversity also supports pollinating insects. Without pollination, many plants would not be able to produce seeds. According to the FAO, about 75 percent of the world's food crops rely on pollinators to reproduce.

Scientists believe there are around 8.7 million species of plants and animals on Earth, with only about 1.7 million of these identified.

HYBRID VS. HEIRLOOM SEEDS

During the 1900s, seed companies focused on developing hybrid varieties of crops that produced larger yields and predictable harvests. Through time, more farmers adopted hybrid seeds and abandoned the traditional **heirloom seeds** they had used for years.

THE SCIENCE OF SEEDS

Although hybrid seeds produced a larger, predictable harvest, they had a significant drawback. The seeds from the hybrid plants did not reliably produce plants with the desired characteristics. As a result, farmers did not save their seeds for the following harvest. Instead, they bought new hybrid seeds from seed companies that promised the characteristics the farmers wanted. Now, the farmers were dependent on the seed companies.

Around 30,00 different plant species are used in medicine.

Unlike hybrid seeds, which are not saved for future crops, heirloom seeds have been saved and passed down from generation to generation of farmers and gardeners. They come from heirloom varieties that are at least 50 years old. Some are much older that 50 years. Heirloom crops often have unique characteristics such as color and shape. They may have a delicious flavor, beautiful color, or impressive size. You can often find different varieties of heirloom tomatoes—Striped German, Green Zebra, Black Krim—at the farmers market. Farmers and gardeners save the seeds from these plants to preserve these unique traits.

TEXT TO **WORLD**

Do you or people you know grow vegetable gardens? Where do you get your seeds from?

They share them with others. Heirloom seeds produce that same vegetable or flower crop each year.

Because they have survived for decades, heirloom varieties are hardy. They also use natural pollination methods—open-pollination—such as birds, insects, or wind to spread pollen from one plant to another. With heirloom varieties, however, the size of the harvest and its timing may be less predictable than with hybrid varieties.

At Svalbard, seeds are kept in aluminum bags.
credit: NordGen/Dag Terje Filip Endresen

As more people use hybrid seeds, heirloom varieties are being lost. Once an heirloom variety is lost, it is gone forever. Therefore, cultivating heirloom varieties is one way to preserve crop and plant diversity. Collecting heirloom seeds each year and participating in the tradition of sharing heirloom seeds with others allows these varieties to grow and thrive. And it preserves crop diversity. Some crop varieties grow better under different growing conditions. Saving and sharing heirloom seeds protects these varieties and ensures they are not lost. One day, heirloom seeds may help farmers and gardeners adapt their crops as climate conditions change.

Take a tour of the National Laboratory for Genetic Resources Preservation. Why is it important to store several of the same samples in different places?

🔎 NLGRP video

THE SCIENCE OF SEEDS

SEED BANKS

Worldwide, about 1,700 seed banks are preserving the genetic diversity of plants for future generations. A seed bank stores seeds from different plant species. The seeds are often kept at low humidity and cold temperatures, about -4 degrees Fahrenheit (-20 degrees Celsius), which helps preserve the seeds so they can grow later if needed. In a seed bank, the seeds are in a vault, which is flood, bomb, and radiation proof, to further protect the valuable seeds.

Trees and plants are crucial to balancing the climate and combatting climate change, as they store carbon.

One of the most biodiverse seed banks in the world is the Millennium Seed Bank in Sussex, England. It holds a collection of more than 2.4 billion seeds that represent about 40,000 plant species. The Millennium Seed Bank holds seeds from native plants from 189 countries and territories.

It also stores almost 16 percent of Earth's wild plant species. In addition, the Millennium Seed Bank has several glass houses where **horticulturists** grow and nurture various plants.

The Millennium Seed Bank in Sussex, England

credit: Patche99z (CC BY SA 3.0)

Between 2011 and 2021, the Millennium Seed Bank worked with several partners on a project to conserve the wild relatives of priority crops such as bananas, beans, peas, carrots, and apples. The project aimed to protect and preserve the world's future food supplies. To achieve this goal, more than 100 scientists collected about 4,500 seed samples from biodiversity centers around the world. These seeds were stored at the seed bank.

In Fort Collins, Colorado, the National Laboratory for Genetic Resources Preservation is one of the largest seed banks in the world. It currently holds more than 500,000 samples of genetic material from nearly 12,000 plant species. It has the space to store up to 1.5 million samples and can preserve about half of them in **cryogenic** tanks.

Visit the Millennium Seed Bank through this video. What does it mean to think about the long term future of plant biodiversity?

🔎 Millennium Seed Bank video

Scientists use seeds from the bank for research and education as well as to prevent and treat disease resistance. The facility also stores genetic material from animals important to agriculture.

Worldwide, about two in five plant species are at risk of extinction. Plant species are threatened by climate change, habitat loss, pollution, pests, and disease. Seed banks are a way to preserve and protect plant species from disappearing forever. Experts and volunteers travel the world to collect seeds for seed banks. The banks also share valuable seeds with each other as another safety measure.

Humans have improved their cultivated crops to feed the world, but not without consequences. Biodiversity has suffered. Earth's plants, animals, and ecosystems may be less able to handle the planet's changing climate and conditions. Yet hundreds of conservation activists and seed preservation groups are actively working to protect and preserve endangered crop species.

ESSENTIAL QUESTION

Why is it important to maintain diversity in our seed supply?

Earth's seeds and the diverse foods they produce have been vital to human history. Saving these endangered seeds will be an essential part of our human future.

SAVE THE
SEEDS!

Many people buy seeds from a garden store. But you don't have to! Every fruit and vegetable you eat has lots of seeds that have the potential to grow into a new plant that makes more fruit and vegetables. Because of hybrid species, the new plant may not look much like the parent plant, but it's still fun to grow!

> **Eat the yummy parts of your vegetable.** After you're finished, scrape the seeds away from the flesh.

> **Let your seeds dry on a paper plate or towel.** This may take several days.

> **You can store your seeds in a container with a tight lid.** They will keep until you're ready to plant them.

> **Fill a pot with soil and bury the seed about a half inch in the soil.** Water it lightly and put it near natural light.

> **What happens?** Does you seed begin to grow? If not, don't be discouraged! Many seeds from vegetables we buy at the grocery store have trouble growing. Seeds from hybrid plants or from vegetables that weren't fully ripened when picked won't be able to grow. Pick a new vegetable and try again!

Consider This!

Do some research at the library or on the internet about how to save seeds from plants you've grown. Some gardeners are able to avoid buying seeds several years in a row!

MAKE A
SEED BALL

TOOL KIT
- air-dry clay (all natural)
- 1 teaspoon
- water
- potting soil
- native plant seeds

Native plants are an essential part of ecosystems. They provide food and shelter for the animals and insects that live in the ecosystem. Their leaves absorb carbon dioxide and release oxygen into the atmosphere. The roots of these plants help keep soil in place and reduce erosion. Encouraging the growth of native plants improves the health of ecosystems and increases biodiversity. Seed balls are one way to spread native plants. Seed balls are a mixture of seeds, soil, and clay. The soil and clay protect the seeds from wind, hot sun, and animals.

❯ If you do not know what plants are native to your area, contact your state's native plant society. It will be able to give you suggestions.

❯ **Roll a small piece of clay (about 1 teaspoon) into a ball shape.** Then, flatten the clay like a small pancake. Moisten each side with water.

❯ **Add about 2 to 3 teaspoons of soil to the flattened clay.** Mix the soil and clay together. Add a little more water if the mixture is too dry.

❯ **Flatten the clay-soil mixture and add 3 to 4 native plant seeds.** Re-form the seed ball. It should be about 1 to 1.5 inches in diameter.

❯ **Put the seed ball on a flat surface and let it dry for 24 hours.**

❯ **After drying, the seed ball is ready for planting.** Gently press the ball into soil in a pot. Leave the top half exposed to air. Water as needed. Enjoy watching the native plants grow!

Consider This!

What role does the native plant you chose have in the local ecosystem? What insects and animals rely on it. How will encouraging the spread of these plants improve the ecosystem?

GLOSSARY

adapt: to change in order to survive.

agriculture: the science or practice of farming.

alpaca: a long-haired, South American mammal.

anthocyanins: blue, violet, or red bitter-flavored pigments in plants.

anthropologist: a scientist who studies humans and human behavior.

antioxidants: substances in food that help fight disease.

archaeologist: a scientist who studies ancient people and their cultures through the objects they left behind.

archipelago: a group of islands.

arsenic: a highly toxic chemical element.

artificial selection: the breeding of plants and animals to produce desired traits.

asexual: reproduction that does not involve any reproductive organs.

autoimmune: related to the body's natural defense system attacking normal cells by mistake.

autonomous: without human contact.

awn: a stiff, bristle-like part attached to a plant.

BCE: put after a date, BCE stands for Before Common Era and counts years down to zero. CE stands for Common Era and counts years up from zero. This book was published in 2024 CE.

biodiversity: the range of different species in an area.

biofuel: a fuel made from living matter, such as plants.

biotechnology: the use of living things to make useful products.

blight: a plant disease typically caused by a fungus.

bran: the hard, outer layer of a wheat kernel.

breed: to develop new types of plants and animals with improved characteristics.

calorie: a unit of energy in food.

carbohydrates: nutrients that are an important source of energy.

carbon: an element found in living things, including plants. Carbon is also found in diamonds, charcoal, and graphite. It combines with oxygen to form carbon dioxide.

carbon dioxide: a gas formed by a chemical reaction, such as the burning of fossil fuels, the rotting of plants and animals, and the breathing out of animals, including humans.

catastrophic: involving or causing large amounts of damage.

center of origin: the region where a crop was originally domesticated.

chaff: the outer husk in grain such as rice or wheat.

chuño: a freeze-dried potato product developed by the Inca people.

civilization: a complex human society.

climate: the long-term weather pattern in a region.

climate change: a change in long-term weather patterns, which can happen through natural or manmade processes.

complementary: completing or enhancing by providing something additional.

conserve: to save or protect something or to use it carefully so it isn't used up.

cornmeal: maize ground into a coarse flour.

cotyledon: the first leaves produced by a seed.

crop rotation: the practice of growing a series of different types of crops in the same area across a sequence of growing seasons to restore the soil's nutrients.

crops: plants grown for food and other uses.

cross-pollinated: a plant pollinated by pollen from a different plant.

cryogenic: at very low temperature.

cultivate: to raise and grow plants for food.

culture: the beliefs and way of life of a group of people, which can include religion, language, art, clothing, food, holidays, tools, and more.

cuneiform: a system of wedge-shaped letters created by ancient civilizations.

currency: something that can be used to trade or pay for goods.

dehydrate: to take the water out of something.

GLOSSARY

deplete: to use up, drain, or empty.

diversity: a range of different people or things.

domesticate: to adapt a plant or animal from a wild state to benefit humans.

dormant: to be in a resting and inactive state.

drought: a long period of dry weather, especially one that damages crops.

ecosystem: a community of living and nonliving things and their environment. Living things are plants, animals, and insects. Nonliving things are soil, rocks, and water.

edible: can be eaten.

elevation: the height of something above sea level. Also called altitude.

embryo: an organism at its earliest stage of development.

endosperm: the part of a seed that acts as a food store for a developing plant embryo, usually containing starch with protein and other nutrients.

environment: everything in nature, living and nonliving, including plants, animals, soil, rocks, and water.

erosion: the gradual wearing away of soil by water or wind.

ethanol: alcohol made from plants that can be used as fuel.

evolution: gradual change across many years.

export: to send goods to another country to sell.

extinction: the death of an entire species so that it no longer exists.

famine: a severe shortage of food resulting in widespread hunger.

fats: nutrients that are essential to give your body energy and support cell function.

ferment: when a substance breaks down through time into another substance, such as grape juice turning into wine.

fertile: good for growing crops.

Fertile Crescent: in ancient times, a semi-circle of land stretching from the Nile River to the Persian Gulf.

fertility: able to produce or reproduce.

fertilize: to add something to soil to make crops grow better.

fiber: the parts of fruits and vegetables that cannot be digested that help the body move food through the digestive system.

flavonoids: natural substances found in fruit and vegetables that have health benefits.

food security: having ongoing access to enough nutritious, affordable food.

forage: to search widely for food.

fungicide: a chemical that destroys fungus.

fungus: a simple organism that is neither plant nor animal and includes mushrooms, yeasts, and molds.

genetic diversity: the variety of genes within a species.

genetic engineering: the process of manipulating genes to alter the appearance and other characteristics of an organism.

genetics: the study of genes and heredity.

genetically modified organism (GMO): an organism whose DNA has been modified.

genome: an organism's complete set of genetic material.

germ: the part of a wheat kernel that sprouts and grows into a new plant.

germinate: to sprout or begin to grow.

germplasm: the seeds, plant parts, and plants that are used for crop research, breeding, and conservation.

gluten: a protein found in certain cereals, especially wheat.

Green Revolution: a time during the twentieth century when changes in agricultural practices resulted in more food being produced.

habitat: the natural area where a plant or animal lives.

harvest: to gather crops.

heirloom seed: a seed from a plant variety that has been around for at least 50 years.

herbicide: a chemical used to kill unwanted plants such as weeds.

herbivore: an animal that eats only plants.

GLOSSARY

hieroglyphs: a written language that uses pictures and symbols to represent words or ideas.

hominy: a food made from ground corn.

horticulturist: an expert in garden cultivation and management.

hull: the tough outer layer of a grain.

humid: having a high level of moisture in the air.

hunter-gatherer: a nomadic person who lives by hunting, fishing, and collecting food.

hybrid: something that is combined from two different things.

hybrid vigor: the improved health and size of a plant that results from combining two different plants.

Ice Age: a period of time when glaciers covered a large part of the earth.

immigrant: a person who comes to live in another country.

inanimate: not having life.

inbred: a pure-breeding strain of plant.

Indigenous peoples: descendants of the earliest known inhabitants of an area who have a special relationship with the land on which they live.

Industrial Revolution: a period during the eighteenth and nineteenth centuries when large cities and factories began to replace small towns and farming.

innovation: a new creation or a unique solution to a problem.

inscription: a carved message.

Irrigation: a system of transporting water through canals, ditches, or tunnels to water crops.

landrace: a locally adapted variety of a species.

leavened: describes bread that includes an ingredient such as yeast that causes the bread to puff and rise.

life cycle: the growth and changes a living thing goes through, from birth to death.

liquor: an alcoholic drink.

livestock: animals raised for food and other uses.

llama: a long-necked, South American pack animal.

maize: a Central American cereal plant, also known as corn.

malnutrition: poor nutrition caused by not eating the right foods.

manure: animal waste.

mature: fully developed.

mechanization: the use of machines to perform work.

migrate: to move from one region to another.

monocropping: the practice of growing a single crop on the same land year after year.

mortality: the condition of being subject to death.

mutation: a change in an organism's genes.

myth: a traditional story that expresses the beliefs and values of a group of people.

natural selection: one of the basic means of evolution in which organisms that are well-adapted to their environment are better able to survive, reproduce, and pass along their useful traits to offspring.

nectar: a sweet fluid made by flowers that attracts insects.

nian gao: a sweet, sticky cake made from rice, traditionally eaten during Chinese New Year celebrations.

nixtamalization: to soak dried maize in a solution to soften the kernel and improve its taste.

nomadic: a lifestyle that involves moving from place to place.

nutrient: a substance in food and soil that living things need to live and grow.

nutrition: the vitamins, minerals, and other things in food that your body uses to stay healthy and grow.

organic: something that is or was living, such as animals, wood, grass, and insects. Also refers to food grown naturally, without chemicals.

organism: something living, such as a plant or an animal.

open-pollinated: when plants are pollinated by bees, moths, birds, bats, and other natural methods.

paddy field: a flat field that floods with water and can be used to grow rice.

parasite: an organism that feeds on and lives in another organism.

pest: a destructive insect or other animal that attacks crops, food, and livestock.

pesticide: a chemical used to kill pests on crops.

photosynthesis: the process by which plants produce food, using light as energy.

pistil: the part of a flower where seeds are produced.

plantation: a large farm where one crop is often grown.

plumule: the part of a plant embryo that forms a shoot.

pollen: a fine, yellow powder produced by flowering plants.

pollination: the process of transferring pollen from the male part of a flower to the female part so that the flower can make seeds.

polyculture: the practice of growing crops together.

polytheistic: believing in many gods.

poverty: without enough income for the basic needs for living.

predator: an animal that hunts and eats other animals.

proteins: nutrients that are essential to the growth and repair of cells in the body.

radicle: the first part of a plant embryo that emerges and forms a root.

reap: to cut or gather a crop or harvest.

reproduce: to make more of something.

ritual: a series of actions often connected with religion.

savanna: a large grassy area with few trees.

scythe: a tool that consists of a long, curved blade on a pole with two handles that is used for cutting grain crops.

sedentary: inactive and spending a lot of time sitting.

seed bank: a place where seeds from different plant species are stored and protected.

selective breeding: the process of breeding plants or animals for specific traits or combinations of traits—a type of artificial selection.

self-pollinated: a plant pollinated by the pollen it produces.

sickle: a sharp farming tool in the shape of a half moon used for cutting grain.

slash-and-burn agriculture: farming that uses fire to clear land for crops.

sow: to plant seeds.

species: a group of living things that are closely related and can produce offspring.

stable: firmly established and not likely to change.

stamen: the part of a flower that produces pollen.

staple food: a food that is an essential part of our diet.

technology: the tools, methods, and systems used to solve a problem or do work.

terrace: a level area cut into a steep slope to provide a flat section to plant crops.

Three Sisters: the Native American practice of planting corn, squash, and beans together.

thresh: to separate wheat grains from the rest of the plant.

till: to turn the soil to control for weeds and pests and to prepare for seeding.

togosh: a traditional Inca food prepared from fermented potato pulp.

toxic: something that is poisonous or harmful.

trait: a specific characteristic of an organism determined by genes or the environment.

tuber: the thick part of the stem, usually developed underground, of certain plants such as potatoes.

uniform: always the same.

unleavened: prepared without using rising agents such as yeast. Unleavened breads are generally flat.

variation: a different form of something.

vegetative propagation: a method of reproduction that uses part of an old plant to grow a new one.

versatile: able to be used in lots of ways.

vigor: health and well-balanced growth.

zongzi: sticky rice dumplings traditionally eaten during the Chinese Dragon Boat Festival.

Metric Conversions

Use this chart to find the metric equivalents to the English measurements in this book. If you need to know a half measurement, divide by two. If you need to know twice the measurement, multiply by two. How do you find a quarter measurement? How do you find three times the measurement?

English	Metric
1 inch	2.5 centimeters
1 foot	30.5 centimeters
1 yard	0.9 meter
1 mile	1.6 kilometers
1 pound	0.5 kilogram
1 teaspoon	5 milliliters
1 tablespoon	15 milliliters
1 cup	237 milliliters

ESSENTIAL QUESTIONS

Introduction: Why do we rely on so few staple crops in a world of agricultural diversity?

Chapter 1: Why did humans start cultivating crops in different parts of the world at about the same time?

Chapter 2: Why is growing GMO food controversial?

Chapter 3: Why is it important for farmers to stay informed about the science of the crops they are planting?

Chapter 4: Why is it important for new varieties of rice to be both tasty and healthy?

Chapter 5: Why do we need to keep seeking new solutions to blight, pests, and other threats to crops?

Chapter 6: Why is it important to maintain diversity in our seed supply?

RESOURCES

BOOKS

Castaldo, Nancy F. *The Story of Seeds: Our Food Is in Crisis: What Will You Do to Protect It?* Houghton Mifflin Harcourt, 2020.

Denton, Michelle, and Tina Kafka. *Genetic Engineering and Genetically Modified Organisms.* Lucent Press, 2019.

Marie, Paula. *The Evolution of Agricultural Technology.* Britannica Educational Publishing in Association with Rosen Educational Services, 2018.

Marquardt, Meg. *12 Things to Know About the Neolithic Age.* 12-Story Library, 2019.

Morlock, Rachael. *Be Smart About GMOs.* Cavendish Square Publishing, 2023.

Napoli, Donna Jo. *Hunger: A Tale of Courage.* Simon & Schuster BFYR, 2019.

WEBSITES

Crop Trust: *www.croptrust.org*

Millennium Seed Bank at Kew Gardens: *kew.org/wakehurst/whats-at-wakehurst/millennium-seed-bank*

National Corn Growers Association: *ncga.com*

National Association of Wheat Growers: *wheatworld.org*

Potato Association of America: *potatoassociation.org*

Svalbard Global Seed Vault: *seedvault.no*

USA Rice Federation: *usarice.com*

SELECTED BIBLIOGRAPHY

Blake, Michael. *Maize for the Gods: Unearthing the 9,000-Year History of Corn.* University of California Press, 2015.

King, Mary Beth. "UNM Researchers Document the First Use of Maize in Mesoamerica." The University of New Mexico, June 3, 2020.

Marton, Renee. *Rice: A Global History.* Reaktion Books, 2014.

Smith, Andrew F. *Potato: A Global History.* Reaktion Books, 2011.

Zabinski, Catherine. *Amber Waves: The Extraordinary Biography of Wheat from Wild Grass to World Megacrop.* University of Chicago Press, 2020.

Zhang, Xiaorong. *The Story of Rice.* Outskirts Press, 2022.

QR CODE GLOSSARY

Page 10: *youtube.com/watch?v=E_Q5LnNlwZs*

Page 15: *blog.ciat.cgiar.org/origin-of-crops*

Page 17: *youtube.com/watch?v=Cdqcs27fPSU*

Page 18: *youtube.com/watch?v=ZA03FrBl_tw*

Page 25: *geography.name/nikolai-vavilov-and-the-origin-of-cultivated-plants*

Page 29: *ourworldindata.org/grapher/maize-yields*

Page 39: *youtube.com/watch?v=RW_GpNciluA*

Page 41: *nativeseeds.org/blogs/blog-news/types-of-corn*

Page 43: *youtube.com/watch?v=XMDnaQ6hFtU*

Page 50: *wheatfoods.org/how-flour-is-milled*

Page 52: *youtube.com/watch?v=8tp7nvAvuwk&t=72s*

Page 56: *wheatfoods.org/resources/wheat-facts/kernel-of-wheat*

Page 71: *youtube.com/watch?v=7LqAJoD-PpA*

Page 73: *youtube.com/watch?v=B1fgO0EvfhE*

Page 76: *youtube.com/watch?v=iYc73eQbq6o*

Page 78: *consumerreports.org/health/food/types-of-rice-to-try-how-to-use-them-a8159704317*

Page 80: *akc.org/expert-advice/dog-breeds/dachshund-history-badger-dog-breed*

Page 86: *youtube.com/watch?v=lYBuY-DnCJc*

Page 89: *youtube.com/watch?v=rtA9vZopc2M*

Page 90: *youtube.com/watch?v=YbTFCh_XdYI*

Page 93: *youtube.com/watch?v=p9qWJ89m-hY*

Page 100: *virtualtourcompany.co.uk/GlobalSeedVault/index.html*

Page 103: *youtube.com/watch?v=pHaYHocP4_Q*

Page 104: *youtube.com/watch?v=_T0Pzh88lHw*

Page 107: *youtube.com/watch?v=AL1GjIObHP8*

Page 109: *youtube.com/watch?v=gAP_JKKg2kE*